UFOS ATTACK EARTH

Accompanied By Warriors From Atlantis, Lost Cities, Living Dinosaurs, And A Bloody Arsed Pirate Or Two

THE OUT OF CONTROL UNIVERSE OF HAROLD T. WILKINS

Edited by Sean Casteel

Introduction by Timothy Green Beckley

Global Communications

This first edition published in 2007 by
Inner Light/Global Communications
Box 753, New Brunswick, NJ 08903

Free Weekly Newsletter at
www.ConspiracyJournal.com

Copyright © 2007 by
Timothy Green Beckley dba Global Communications

Editor: Sean Casteel
www.seancasteel.com

Cover Design By
TIM SWARTZ

Inside Art By
CAROL ANN RODRIGUEZ

PRESIDENT AND PUBLISHER
TIMOTHY GREEN BECKLEY

CONTENTS

1. The Out Of Control Universe Of Harold T. Wilkins .... - 5 -

2. Dreaming of Hidden Treasure and the Occasional Ghost .... - 9 -

3. A Bloody-Arsed Pirate Or Two .... - 17 -

4. Warriors Of Atlantis .... - 25 -

5. The Destruction of Atlantis .... - 29 -

6. A Ghostly Underground World .... - 35 -

7. Strange Creatures and Monsters Galore .... - 41 -

8. Dinosaurs Haunt America .... - 47 -

9. More American Dinosaurs .... - 55 -

10. King Kong Lives! .... - 61 -

11. Anthropoids, Giants and Mammoths .... - 69 -

12. Live Monsters And Other Creatures Of Africa .... - 75 -

13. Fearsome Creatures Great And Small .... - 81 -

14. Monstrous and Strange They Are .... - 87 -

15. Bat-Like Creature Seen Over California .... - 93 -

16. The Martian Cat Among The Pigeons .... - 99 -

17. Tales Of An Alien Death Ray And Explosions In The Sky .... - 107 -

18. Are The UFO Occupants Midgets? .... - 115 -

19. Flying Saucers Of Ancient Days .... - 121 -

20. Flying Saucer Humanoids Vs. The Space Monsters .... - 127 -

21. The Woman From Behind The Moon .... - 135 -

22. The Magic Venusians .... - 143 -

23. Tales of Teleportation .... - 151 -

24. Monster Of Mystery And A Strange Skeleton .... - 159 -

25. Quantum Physics And Bizarre Animals .... - 165 -

26. A Final Vanishing Act .... - 173 -

27. The Great Unknown .... - 177 -

The Out Of Control Universe Of Harold T. Wilkins

By Timothy Green Beckley

It was admittedly a toss-up.

Did I use that quarter to get a double-dip cone (and get change back), or put that twenty-five cent piece into an envelope and send it off to the address in back of the comic? The ice cream would offer immediate satisfaction, but in the long run wouldn't I be better off waiting for the mailman to deliver a copy of what seemed to be the most incredible offering a preteen boy could wish for?

The publisher was E. Haldeman-Julius, and the ad made it sound like I was going to receive a big thick book for my meager investment. I mean, with a title like **Monsters and Mysteries of America, the Jungles, the Tropics, and the Arctic Wastes**, how could I know the offering would turn out to be a 30-page booklet? The publisher had further tempted me with the intriguing subtitle: "Strange Stories of Modern Adventures Suggesting That The King Kongs And The Dinosaurs May Still Be Alive Today."

It was a mouthful, and it stole my breath away.

The author was Harold T. Wilkins, whom I knew nothing about. There was no bio on him in the book to hint at his credentials. He had to be the first Crypto-zoologist—years before I even knew what a Crypto-zoologist was.

Despite the size of the publication, the information I was about to consume could be termed magical. True, the stories the author related were teasers. Tidbits to whet a fertile imagination: living dinosaurs, gigantic birds, mastodons being hunted in our lifetime. Giant apes larger than King Kong. And sex between normal women and giant hairy humanoids.

Who was this Harold T. Wilkins that was making my head swim and my flesh crawl?

UFOs Attack Earth... The Out of Control Universe of Harold T. Wilkins

As it turns out, Harold T. Wilkins was a Brit who was born in 1891 and educated at Cambridge. (I don't have any idea if he graduated or not.) Nothing is known about his youth, at least as far as I could find out, and his first literary efforts center around the much-maligned pioneer of early television John L. Baird, a UK inventor who Wilkins struck up a correspondence with. Some of their letters can be found in the files of the Library of the University of British Columbia.

I guess we can ascertain from this that Wilkins had an interest in "fringe" science, which those of that era most positively would have considered the idea of sending moving pictures through the air. At the very least, Wilkins certainly could be thought a trendsetter. In other words, he had a head for being ahead of his time.

We really can't say how much traveling Wilkins did in order to research a topic. His first books were on pirates. ***Captain Kidd and Skeleton Island,*** inked in 1937, was followed three years later by ***Panorama of Pirate Treasure***. The book on Captain Kidd is well over 300 pages and reveals a "secret code" the rum-drinking swashbuckler is said to have created that holds clues to the whereabouts of his booty—thus the bloody-arsed pirate in this book's elongated title.

It seems natural that the next category Wilkins set out to conquer was the mysteries of the seas. I've never seen a copy of ***Mysteries and Monsters of the Deep***, penned in 1948, but I am certain it would be a nice read.

Around this same period of the late 1940s and early 50s, Harold fancied himself a world explorer. We don't know for sure if he ever ventured into the jungles in search of lost civilizations, but he did freak out his readers with stories of Atlantis, pyramids and unknown tribes and races hidden away from civilization. ***Ancient South America***, written in 1945, was followed by ***Secret Cities of Old South America*** in 1952, both of which appear to draw heavily on the style and ideology of Madame Blavatsky, the founder of the Theosophy Society.

As the years marched on, Wilkins appears to have gone back and checked out the works of Charles Fort. In fact, his ***Flying Saucers On The Moon*** and ***Flying Saucers On The Attack*** (1954) lean a great deal up upon Fort's original research. Wilkins was a colorful writer, and so he colored up much of the material he found, whether it was in someone else's book or in the local press. It can safely be said that Wilkins added flavor and spice as he went along, thus kicking up a notch material that might have otherwise been dull and lackluster. He was appealing to a generation weaned on movie cliffhangers and radio dramatizations. He did what he had to do—present this material in a colorful, thought-provoking manner.

The result? His books sold in the tens of thousands, mainly to an eager, youthful audience. Some consider his works on UFOs to be "potboilers," and though they may not carry much in the way of defined reference points, they are our written legacy of the earliest Ufological days when the subject had not yet been overly contaminated by whackos and those bent on pushing their own "rock solid" ideals.

Harold T. Wilkins passed away in 1960, but he left us with a reservoir of data to ponder and ponder again. His influence on the field of the paranormal is greater than most people realize. Almost everyone interested in the strange and unexplained has no doubt picked up a book by Wilkins and absorbed its contents, nodding their head in approval when reading some of the accounts in them, and perhaps snickering at other tales which they might feel are too contrived or too damn far out to take at face value.

The world has revolved around the sun many, many times since Wilkins joined up with the crew of that great mothership in the sky. We offer this work to those who may not have had the opportunity to read his offerings, and who wish to evoke his spirit now, and to those who wish to recall his writing in the fondest of ways.

God only knows that the Universe will never be the same!

UFOs Attack Earth... The Out of Control Universe of Harold T. Wilkins

Dreaming of Hidden Treasure and the Occasional Ghost

We begin with some stories taken from one of Harold T. Wilkins' earliest books, called *Panorama of Treasure Hunting*, published in 1940. These particular treasure stories all have supernatural overtones, the kind that offer chills along with the thrills of the proverbial search for gold. They also show Wilkins' razor-sharp sense of humor and uncanny ear for dialogue and ring with an old English authenticity that is a sheer delight to read.

A DREAM COMES WITH MUCH PURPOSE

The old Brito-Roman town of Uriconium (or Wroxeter, near Shrewsbury, England) is the locale of another old woman's lucky dream. It happened in the 1870s, and she was dame Betty Fox, wife to a wheelwright. Bet spent a lot of her time grubbing about in old Roman ruins, and daydreaming about finding Roman gold. She had no luck, and the peering grannums in her village had a lot of fun about old Betty's "maggots." But the more they laughed, the more did she. One night, the luck turned: she dreamt she saw a crock of gold buried, under an alder-bush, on a bank on one side of the lane leading from Wroexeter to the old Horse Shoe Inn. The lane cut very deeply through high ground on which the ancient Roman town had once stood. Round there, the best Roman houses had been located, and the banks, just here, are very high and descend much below the level of the ancient Roman floors.

UFOs Attack Earth... The Out of Control Universe of Harold T. Wilkins

Bet woke her husband and told him; but he snorted and cursed her for waking him out of his own dreams of bliss in the bowery, and bade her turn round and go to sleep again. She did, and the same dream rose again before her. Up Bet rose, and without waking her snoring husband, doffed shift and pulled on long black cotton stockings and skirt and apron, and, lifting some tools from her husband's wicker frail, walked out of the cottage into the lane, but not so pussyfooted as she might have been. It was around 3 A.M., and the predawn light was yellowing the wan eastern sky. Yet, early as it was, that did not prevent another poke-nosing old girl from raising her own window sash and presenting a vision of frowsy nightcap, and a dirty shift that barely concealed some rather monstrous charms. Her eyes goggling, the old girl opened her mouth and bawled an inquiry from cackling lips that cause neighboring dogs to howl in protest.

"Aye, Mother Fox, and where ye be bound to this time o' night?"

Mother Fox responded with a saucy touch of her hand on a stern view of her own posteriors, followed by some derisive advice.

"No wonder yer old man has to rise early in the morning, with so light a sleeper at his side. I am off where 'twill do no good to tell ye. I've dreamt it, at last, in gold."

"Garn, ye trollopsing, traipsing old swatchel. Ye orter be washin' yer old man's durty shirts, and not waking decent folk up at this unearthly time 'o the marning, a strollin' round the country like some old hooer (whore)."

Saying which, the lady with the monstrous charms banged the window down and went "chundering" back to bed.

Bet ignored the insult and went on to the alder-tree. She had no trouble in locating it. She dug and turned up on the prongs of her fork an ancient earthenware urn, which broke into pieces, and out rolled a heap of silver coins. Gathering them into her apron, Bet hurried home; but her coming was not missed by the lady in the shift, whose suspicions had become excited. She threw up the window and was greeted with a triumphant shout from Bet.

"The old hooer's found it!"

"Eh, what?" bawled the old lady, shrilly.

"My a . . ." was the reply. Bet had prepared a choice bon mot, which, as Dean Swift, of St. Patrick's Dublin, tells us, used to be very popular among smart ladies of quality in his day, when some indiscreet fellow had been induced to "buy it." Back in the cottage, Bet emptied her hoard into a pie dish, while her husband's mouth opened.

"Ha, call me a fool dista? Oo's the fool, thee or me?"

Mr. Fox wisely forebore answering this Socratic inquiry. The coins were in good condition. The finder got about $200 for them. Bet had a son who inherited her faculty, and, in excavation work, he often left a spot where an archeologist bade him dig and chose one about which he dreamt the night before.

A MACABRE DREAM

In many of these occult stories of treasure hunting, one finds that human blood must be shed before the hog-boy of the cache comes across with the boodle. A macabre story of this sort was located in the garrison town of Semendria, in old Serbia, about the year 1880. Here, a corporal, Ilia Konstantinovicz dreamt, several times running, that an immense treasure was hidden in the tower of the fortress. Blood from the heart of a man had first to be sprinkled on the place before the treasure would come out of the cache. The heart had to be replaced in the body, and the searchers would find an iron coffer containing a colossal fortune, and a bottle containing an "elixir vitae" guaranteed to make the dead man come to life and dance with tears in his eyes.

The credulous corporal told the secret to a comrade, one Radulovicz, and begged him to offer himself as victim! R. took some convincing that he was the right man for this delicate job. He felt it might be awkward for both, if the mystic tonic in the bottle did not answer the promises of the mystic advertisement. Seeing no help for it, the corporal offered himself as victim. So, one Sunday night, at 11 P.M., the two gunners quitted the fort and went to the alleged cache. The corporal, repeating his instructions, undressed and cut his own throat with a knife he had sharpened for the purpose. The shuddering soldier dug all night, but found nothing and in the cold dawn fainted. The guard found him and brought him before the adjutant, where other soldiers corroborated his story.

UFOs Attack Earth ... The Out of Control Universe of Harold T. Wilkins

A VOICE SHRIEKING AS HE DUG

In the year 1821, there was alive at St. Just, Cornwall, an old chap who held spellbound, on wintry nights in the village alehouse, a Cornish audience listening to his yarn of a ghostly adventure on a Cornish moor. When he had well whetted his pipes and plugged his churchwarden pipe with some good tobacco, presented to him, he started:

"You all do know the ruins 'o that old chapel above Cape Cornwall, as they calls Chapel Carnbrea, and you do all know the little hillocks that surround it like graves in a churchyard? Hee hee, how you do all shudder!"

His hard-baked audience of wreckers and smugglers who cared for poor shipwrecked seamen no more than they did for our Lord the King and his English revenue officers, shuddered and muttered about "pixies a-haunting they ruins."

"Well, them mounds be graves of Druid priests and ancient kings of Cornwall, and it is said their riches were buried wi' them, but nobody had pluck enough to disturb they ruins. I wanted money badly; so one night, soon after I came here to live, I shoulders me pick and shovel and hikes over the down towards the old ruins. I picked out the biggest mound and dug, hoping to find gold. The earth on top was easy to work, but the deeper down I got, the harder it got to work. Several hours passed, and I was a-sweatin' like a bull in a medder, and had got down only several feet when dawn were right close. It be a lonely spot to be workin' in the dead of the night. I could hear the waves, below, as they broke against the tall cliffs under the cape, and sometimes, it seemed to me as I could hear dead men's voices slyly calling to me under the sea. My hair began to raise and my courage oozed clean away.

"I swigged several times of the brandy bottle in me pouch, and ses to meself: 'Ah, Tom, wi' all that gold below, the divill himself can't frighten ye off it!' Presently the dawn lit the sky and I went home, meaning to return next night and finish the job. I knew nobody 'ood venture up there to disturb my work, not if they could help it! And I didn't want to be seen workin' there in the daytime. Gets a feller a bad name to be seen a-disturbin' old graves! But I knew the sight of an open grave 'ood keep all priers away, even if they were bold enough to come so near as to see it.

"Next night I was on the spot with me tools, a-diggin'. To my astonishment, the grave was filled up! There was nothing to explain it. Not a soul to be seen. I puts spade to earth and heaves away till I come to the hard soil again. I worked harder than any man ever worked for his living till, at last, my spade touches something hard. Might be a rock. I cleared the earth all around it, and came on a large stone slab, cut with queer letters. It sounded hollow, when I tapped me pick on it. The moon shone bright into the grave, and I saw the figures cut into the stone. Under this, then, was the coffin and the treasures. I tried to lever up the slab, but it beat me. Clearly, the pit would have to be much bigger and wider, and even then, it looked as if four gurt, strong men couldn't raise that stone, heave as they might. I clambered down into the grave, which was now deep enough to hide me from sight. Suddenly a horrific shriek sounded overhead. I stood up, expecting to see some night prowler come tumbling into the hole; but when I got on me hands and knees and looked around over the edge of the hole, there wa'n't a soul there! I had to leave off again, and when I come back, again, the grave was filled in . . . .

"'Oho, Tom,' says I to meself, 'third time's lucky time. I'll ha' that there gold if I dies for it!' Down I went, swearing at the work undone, and again reached the stone slab. This time I widened and lengthened the grave at each end. I drove the point of me pick in the stone slab and was about to prise it up, when the same horrid shriek sounded, and a shower of earth fell all around me, in the hole. Like lightning, I scrambled out of that pit, for I didn't want to be buried alive, and as I got on top of the mound of earth I had raised, I see a grey figure moving swiftly away—but whether man or woman, imp or demon out of hell, Lord alone knows. At that moment, me toe slipped out of the notch I had made and I falls headlong into that grave, causing another shower of earth. I scrambled out as best I could and went home. I'd had enough on it. I felt I should never get that treasure out."

THE GHOST IN WILD WALES

Wild Wales has many ghost-guarded caches. Powis Castle, for example, used to be haunted by the picturesque figure of a white-bearded, flowing-haired seneschal, in embroidered breaches and costume of the late middle ages. One night, he ungallantly visited the bedroom of a needlewoman—your medieval ghost is by no means backward in entering ladies' bedrooms, unasked, as, doubtless, was his way when in life! He bent down, looked in her face, and when she woke, stifling a scream, he beckoned to her to arise in her nightie and follow him. (As it was an early Victorian wrapper, with convoluted trowsers at the end, we may suppose it was proof against the night air and the draughts in old castle corridors.) She followed him down the echoing corridor, with the squeaking oaken staircase, into a tapestried chamber; not even staying in the way to glance into a pier glass. Suddenly, the aged specter halted, bent down, and lifted up a board. He tugged out a dusty, heavily banded iron chest.

"Thee art to tell the Earl of Powis, woman," said he, and vanished.

The needlewoman duly told the Earl, who took out the chest, laden with title deeds and valuable jewels of a fourteenth-century pattern. The needlewoman was rewarded "according to her station in life."

THE YOUNG LADY'S EXERTIONS

A wistful poltergeist made his appearance, at a house in Petersfield, Hampshire, in January 1931. It is an old, three-roomed cottage, in which live a gardener and his handsome, twenty-year-old daughter. They were disturbed by frequent rappings, and it seemed the noises used to follow the daughter around the house. (Maskelyne, the magician, is not alone in ascribing falls of furniture, which happen in such cases, not always to apparitions, but to some mysterious force of nature, often unconsciously exerted by a young woman or girl.)

The daughter began to try to talk with the ghost; much as the Comte de Mirville, about a century earlier, had opened up communications with a similar alleged spook, in a Norman French house. Said she: "Tap thrice for 'Yes,' and once for 'No.'" The "ghost" responded.

The code established, the girl proceeded to ask the rapper, who he had been in life. He remained obstinately silent. Then she tapped out the question: "Have you concealed money here?"

"Yes," came the answer.

"Will you show us where?"

UFOs Attack Earth . . . The Out of Control Universe of Harold T. Wilkins

The ghost went rapping along the wall till he reached the fireplace in a downstairs room. He stopped, and rapped "Yes" on the hearthstone. The gardener prised up a flag, but treasure he found none. That night, in disgust, the angry Poltergeist hurled a glass to the floor and elevated a bed—but not, so I understand—the pretty young lady's bed, though, really, we would not "put it past him!" As there are only three rooms in the cottage, it should not need much time to find the buried gold, and time, as all hunters know, is of the essence of these contracts. Both a vicar and a local police chief say they have heard the rapper, rapping from the boundaries of an unseen world.

UFOs Attack Earth . . . The Out of Control Universe of Harold T. Wilkins

A Bloody-Arsed Pirate Or Two

The following story is also taken from Harold T. Wilkins' *Panorama of Treasure Hunting*. Wilkins recounts a story told to him by a seaman acquaintance he identifies only as J.W., who tells Wilkins how he came into possession of a gun once owned by a pirate named Henry Avery. From that starting point, Wilkins narrates a stirring, classic tale of 17th century pirating, complete with the capture of loot and women from a Moslem trading ship, as well as Avery's poignant beginnings and later attempts to clear himself of charges of piracy. While Avery claimed that he never intended any harm to a fellow Englishman, he was nevertheless skinned alive in Old Bristol, England, in 1696.

CAPTAIN AVERY'S SILVER-MOUNTED PISTOL

One hot morning, two weeks after we had come ashore in Frigate Island, I was lying on my back, tired out, in the shadow of the northern cliffs of the cove, keeping a wary eye for any of the evil-eyed land crabs, who had holes in the base of these cliffs. My eyes wandered along the basalt and sandstone, streaking the cliffs of the headland; when, all of a sudden, I started in surprise, and raised myself onto my elbow. The skipper lay close by, huddling in the shelter of a fire of green twigs, which he had made to keep off the "pinging" mosquitoes and midges.

"Say, captain, look here!" I shouted.

"What's up now? You ain't found a barrel with a million gold dollars in it, 'ave you, now?" he snorted, hardly looking my way.

"No," I replied, " but if you look hard at that cliff yonder, you will see, as the light strikes it, a faint arrow pointing downwards."

"By ___, so 'tis," shouted the captain, now all excitement. Hands heard the shout and came running up. They all began to dig furiously in the sands of the cove at the base of the cliffs, to which the arrow pointed. We made the sand fly, I can tell you! About five feet down, we came on the sides of a rotten chest, so decayed that the boards fell to pieces as our picks touched them. Inside the chest was an old coat—very old fashioned in style and cut—and under it, a waistcoat, with remarkably big pewter buttons. The cloth, too, was rotten as punk. There were, in the chest, several old battered rings, made of a peculiarly reddish gold. And there was a pistol—an ancient one—as rusty as an old horseshoe on a barn door.   The pistol has a butt, handsomely mounted in silver, and on it is a plate, engraved, and looking quite as old as the pistol itself. The inscription reads: "CAPTn Avery His Barker." (I can find no use of the word *barker* earlier than about the middle of the 18th century, when footpads and highwaymen on the toby—the old counterparts of the modern American hijackers—applied it to their pistols. May be, then, some seaman of the 18th century buried this pistol in Cocos Island? *Author.*)

We hunted round and dug up every inch of the sand, within a radius of fifty feet and more; but I deeply regret to say we did not find any major cache to which this chest may have been a pointer. Nor did we discover any clue to the identity of the men who buried this chest in Wafer's Cove. I am going back to that island, someday, to make another search.

(HAROLD T. WILKINS' NOTE: *The seaman who had the adventure, told above, was, when I last heard of him, on a voyage in a tramp steamer, outward-bound to China. As he said, when he came to the house of a collector friend of mine, who lives in Sussex coast of England: "That blasted island is as wet as a bleedin' sponge, with rain, rain, everlastin' rain. The others kept the battered rings of gold, and I had the pistol, which I am willing to sell you. I saw an old portrait in oils, done of Sir Henry Morgan, the buccaneer. It hangs in the old café in Panama, but the Dago landlord wouldn't sell to me. But I'll let you have the old powder horn, and the pistol of Avery, the bloody pirate."*)

UFOs Attack Earth . . . The Out of Control Universe of Harold T. Wilkins

It is possible that that old and rotten chest may have been the clue to the major cache; and of course, on the other hand, it may not. In the days of the conquest in Spanish Mexico and another parts of Latin Central America, arrows on the walls of canons were often used to indicate the place where gold had been concealed. Sometimes, the arrows were so placed that they were visible only on a certain day, or month, or at some hour when the sunshine struck at a particular angle, onto the walls of the cliff. Round old Texas and the Rio Grande, and in the wilder gorges of Colorado, I have known arrow-markings to be found in just these conditions of light or shadow.

Assuming that this pistol was part of the armory of the notorious pirate, it would be interesting to know how it came to be hidden in a chest in a cove of Cocos Island. No one knows that Avery, any more than Captain William Kidd, ever landed in Cocos Island; though in both cases, they met men who *had* visited Cocos; Avery, who died in misery and want at Bideford, Devon, in 1699, was skinned alive by rapscallion and "godlie" merchants, of old Bristol City. *They* were land pirates whom the law protected, and who made it all right with God, by endowing or bequeathing money to churches, in which they had their aldermanic family pews.

DRIVEN TO A LIFE OF CRIME

There is some uncertainty about the social origin of Avery. His father died when the son was aged ten; whereupon a villainous uncle robbed the nephew of money and land, and put him apprentice to a brutal sea captain. The uncle hoped that this Captain Tarpowling would made short work of this brass bounder, but it so happened that the brass bounder, young Avery, lived to make short work of other people. He is said to have joined the Royal Navy and to have served under Sir Edward Spragge, at the bombardment of piratical Algiers, in 1671. It is likely, therefore, that Avery met, in this squadron, both Captain William Kidd and the famous Dampier, who, too, had been impressed to serve his sad majesty, King Charles II.

Avery, discharged without pension or pay, went a-buccaneering in the Caribbean. He is described as a fat and jolly man, daring and good-natured; but not one to forgive an imposition easily. In his red and merry face, you could see, with half an eye, what was his "jolly trade." He was a good mathematician and, also, by way of an English patriot, with moral principles.

A thirteen-year-old cabin boy of his, one, Philip Myddleton, of Prescot Street in Goodman's fields, later on, a King's evidence man in the trial of Avery's old pirates, told the judges in Doctor's Commons, old London, of a fine letter which Avery left at Johanna, the old black bawds' and lemon boozer's island, so well known to both honest and piratical "lime-juicers," in the South Indian Ocean, off the coast of East Africa. The blackamoor chief, there, was to deliver to the first English ship that came in, this letter:

"To all English commanders, Let this satisfy you and all concerned yet there was riding here, ye 18th February 1695, the ship *Fancy* man-of-war. I never yet wronged any English or Dutch, or ever so intend while I command. Wherefore, as I commonly speak with all ships, I desire all who peruse this to take this signal following: If any of you, or whom you may inform, are desirous to know what we are from a distance, then make up your ancient in a ball and hoist them at your mizzen peak, leaving your peak ensign unfurled. I shall answer with ye same, and never molest you if it be possible. But my men are hungry, stout and resolute, and should they exceed my desire I may not help myself. AS YET A FRIEND TO ALL ENGLISHMEN. Given at Johanna, ye 18th February 1695, Henry Avery."

PILLAGING AND RAPING AS THEY WENT

Avery's blades lay off Mocha, in Arabia, for a month; waiting for the coming of the Indian Mogul Emperor's ships, bringing the gold and silver, gained by the sale of Indian goods taken by the annual Indian Moslem pilgrims, bound to Mecca. The pirates burnt the Arabian seaport town, and blew up the mosque; and then made off on the track of the ***Gunsway***, or the Mogul ship, ***Gang-I-Sawai***, which had gone by them in the dark of the night. They came up with her and met with stern resistance from Captain Ibrahim Khan, who fought with the name of Allah, in his mouth, and with the sight of the prophet's scimitar flashing before his eyes. The fight raged on, ding-dong, for two hours. The Indian ship had 1300 people aboard; the pirates, 104 Englishmen, including nine West countrymen, 14 Danes, and 52 Frenchmen. A gun burst in the Mogul's ship, and the pirate's shot smashed her mainmast; whereon, in the confusion, the Indian captain rushed down into the hold of the *Gunsway* and did a rather odd thing. He clapped turbans on the heads of some lovely Turkish odalisques, whom he intended for his harem in India, and bade them fight; but beauty was no match for the arms of the bearded English and other pirates, swearing like old Falstaff, when the landlord would give him no more tick for his wine or sack.

The pirates looted the ship, got great quantities of jewels, and a saddle and bridle, set with jewels, sent from the Emir of Mecca to the Mogul, in Delhi. Several of the Indian women were richly dressed and seemed to be of "quality." But most of the treasure eluded the pirates; since not even torture would make the brave Lascars and Hindus reveal where it was hidden, in the Mogul's great ship.

Khufi Khan, a Mogul historian, says the pirates stripped the dead of their jewels and money and raped the Indian women. More than one high-born Moslem lady of Hindostan, threw herself into the sea, or fell on the knives of the pirates, rather than yield herself to the embraces of the bearded, swearing devils of Avery's pirate squadron. The pirate cabin boy, Philip Myddleton, says merely that the pirates lay with the women onboard; but does not make clear their eventual fate.

For years after his death, Captain Avery, like Captain Kidd, was specially excerpted from every proclamation in which the Lord Chief Justice, or the King, promised free pardons to bloody pirates, who turned from the evil of their ways and reformed. It is likely that some old member of Avery's pirate ship, the *Fancy*, took the captain's silver-mounted "barker" to Cocos Island.

After Captain Avery's pirates in the *Fancy* had plundered the Great Mogul's ship, the *Gunsway*, they (says tradition), fled towards Madagascar; shared out the plunder, at from 700 pounds to 1000 pounds a man (a large amount of money in those days); raped the Mogul's princess daughter and her high-born ladies; and, (as colonial archives show), sailed for the Bahamas—at that time a notorious rendezvous of some of the worst pirates and old buccaneers in the Caribbean. At old Providence, in the Bahamas, a scoundrel of a Colonial governor, (Nicholas Trott) then appointed by a semi-private board of Lords Proprietors, accepted the ship *Fancy*, and pirate loot, from Captain Avery; gave him a passport; and saw him sail for England in another "boughten" ship, the *Sea Flower*.

UFOs Attack Earth . . . The Out of Control Universe of Harold T. Wilkins

Captain Avery and thirty of his old pirates landed in Ireland. The captain and his men found themselves in Dublin, when a proclamation came out, calling for their apprehension. Avery absconded by water, to Devonshire, and hid in Bideford (as stated). There was now a general scattering of Avery's old pirates. Ireland had become too hot to hold them. Some got aboard a packet boat and landed in West Wales; others found themselves on the shores of Devon, where they no sooner landed than they had "to hot-foot" across the countryside. Even so, many of them were laid by the heels. There was a hue and cry out! Strange seamen, with earrings and tattooed hairy chests, fetching out queer gold coins, to pay for tavern scores in Devon "boozers," became suspect. Many a man wished he had never seen "Rabbin gold," or had been left ashore, naked, on some island in the coral seas, ere he came before the portentous red-robed hang-'em-out-of-hand judges of King William's day!

To say truth, not all the absconders were captured in the lanes of Devon, on the hills and in the coves of Somerset, or in the wild mountains of Wales. Nay, some of them gave leg bail to our Sovereign Lord the King, his judges and his constables and justices. It may be that one of them, one who had escaped through the very wide meshes of justice in Dutch William's day, got across the broad and roaring seas with his plunder, including this silver-mounted pistol of the Captain. And, subsequently, he may have buried it in the sands of the cove of Cocos Island, in the North Pacific, where, two hundred and twenty-seven years later, it was found and dug up by my old friend and shipmate, "J.M."

All this, of course, is conjecture. What a pity that the pistol cannot speak and tell its own tale, so much better than my speculations, or the legends of the Cocos Islands syndicates.

UFOs Attack Earth . . . The Out of Control Universe of Harold T. Wilkins

Warriors Of Atlantis

In a 1945 book called *Mysteries of Ancient South America*, Wilkins writes a great deal about the Lost Continent of Atlantis, including the little-known history of a race of Atlantean warriors bent on world conquest. Their brutal militarism quite negatively impacts on Atlantis itself, and the gods eventually punish the warrior race by totally destroying their homeland. Wilkins compares certain aspects of the situation to that of England in the days of World War II, which was still going on when he wrote the material that follows.

EVIL WERE THE DAYS

On earth, the times were disturbingly like the present. Disharmony and disunity reigned over the planet. Live and let live was an outmoded and despised principle. There was a great world war raging. Psenophis, the old priest of Heliopolis, showed the secret temple archives, concerning the story of this ancient and forgotten world war, to Solon, the Greek, visiting the Nile about 537 B.C. The old Egyptian priest said the catastrophe happened 9000 years before. A race of militarists had sailed out of the Atlantic and invaded all Western Europe and Northern Africa, as far as Libya's deserts. They had a large navy and army. Paying no heed to any nations desiring, in that far-off day, to remain neutral, they overran every country between Gibraltar and the modern Lavant, till they finally confronted one army alone: that of an ancient Attican race of probable Pelasgian origin. These ancient men of a forlorn hope of freedom stood in much the same position as did Britain, in 1940, at bay behind her moat, and defying the armies of Hitler, who had also overrun most of Europe.

"The earth was corrupt and full of violence . . . the wickedness of man was very great in the earth . . . every imagination of his heart was only evil continually." (So Genesis, drawing on some extremely ancient, pre-Babylonian source, long lost.)

WAR IS HELL

Militarism and rage for conquest had made a hell both of Atlantis and, according to the old Sansar legends, of the land in the Pacific called Rutas (Lemuria), where black and yellow races struggled perpetually. Aelianus Glaudas, the Roman rhetor, who died A.D. 410, cites a very curious story about conditions in Atlantis prior to the great cataclysm. It is taken from a vanished book of the great Greek historian Theopompus, who flourished at Chios, in 354 B.C. Only a few fragments of the histories of Theopompus have survived, and in one of them there is a very curious talk between a certain Silenus and Midas. [Wilkins gives his own translation from the Latin.]

"Europe and Asia and Libya (Africa), islands, are girdled by the ocean. Beyond them are continents of infinite size, which support great animals, and men double our size, and span of years. In the same are great cities, with laws and customs of a life wholly different from ours. This land possesses great quantities of gold and silver, which are reckoned by these people as of less value than iron is with us. Among these cities are the two greater than the rest: one named Machimus, the other Eusebius. They are quite unlike. Machimus is warlike; Eusebius is pious and peace loving. The peace loving people reap the fruits of the earth without plows or oxen. They have no need to sow or till. As he said, they live free from sickness and die laughing, and with great pleasure. They are so exactly just that the gods many times vouchsafe to converse with them. The other inhabitants are continually armed and fighting, and subdue their neighbors. Sometimes they die of sickness, but this rarely happens. Most commonly they are killed in war, by stones or wood, for they are invulnerable to steel."

JUDGEMENT ON THE WARLIKE

There follows a story of a great invasion of Europe by the warlike race of this Atlantean continent, and two people, named Marcellin and Avienus, make statements about this great island continent.

UFOs Attack Earth . . . The Out of Control Universe of Harold T. Wilkins

Says Marcellin, "In the Atlantic sea, in the European sphere, is a more worthy island."

He is capped by Avienus, who seems to refer to America.

"Fruitful in the ocean stretch lands and beyond and backwards, other shores stretch to another world . . ."

This battle of Atlantean warriors and "old Greeks" figured on a peplos, or embroidered robe, which used to be carried round, in Plato's own day, in the harbor streets of Athens, at a festival of the goddess Athena. One old Greek writer, named Grantor, who lived in 310 B.C., says he actually was shown pillars, in a temple by the Nile, where the Egyptian priests said there was pictured, in hieroglyphics, the history of the drowned continent of Atlantis.

Naturally, however, had the pre-Diluvian age man been good or evil, man of a golden age or necromancer of a race of half-demons, he could not have prevented the impact of that wandering, cosmic body from outer space. "What had to be had to be"; for, as the Greeks themselves said, not even the gods on the high hill of violet-crowned Olympus can deflect by a hair the decrees of death and destiny.

It may be, as Mr. H.G. Wells contends, that history never repeats herself in an infinitely varied and incessant universe; but on this occasion, at least, as old Lord Palmerston might have said, she "came damned near it."

Suddenly, without warning, as the two embattled armies confronted each other, there came, as the ancient Egyptian records said: "violent earthquakes and floods, and, in a single night and day of misfortune, all the warlike men in a body sank into the ground, and the island of Atlantis disappeared into the depths of the sea."

The old priest Psonchis, of the Egyptian temple of Thais (or Sais), made a further remarkable statement: "There was a rain of fire from the skies, caused by a declination of astronomical bodies moving around the sun and in the heavens. The great conflagration recurs at long intervals, and those who live on high mountains and lofty places are more liable to destruction than people by rivers or seashore."

UFOs Attack Earth . . . The Out of Control Universe of Harold T. Wilkins

The Destruction of Atlantis

This chapter is also taken from *Mysteries of Ancient South America,* and consists mainly of a description of the destruction of Atlantis seen from the perspective of more primitive peoples on the periphery of that earlier Apocalypse, like the Bushmen of the Kalahari Desert. Wilkins summons up a poetic but terrifying vision of what the cataclysm would have been like to the distant observer, but the section closes on a note of hope. It should be noted that before writing *Mysteries of Ancient South America*, Wilkins actually traveled to that continent by steamship shortly before the outbreak of World War II in the hope of verifying some of his theories about Atlantis having left colonies behind in unexplored parts of Brazil and elsewhere in South America.

THE EARTH'S GREATEST DISASTER

In this book, I find it necessary to start at the end, rather than the beginning; since there are many intelligent people who have to be convinced that this cataclysm told in a rather naïve and garbled form, in Genesis, and certainly no myth actually occurred and was no merely local catastrophe of what is now called Iraq.

Twelve thousand years ago, not more than a short hour in the long history of our planet, the ancestors of the fast-vanishing Bushmen dwarfs of the Kalahari Desert of South Africa were cowering in terror behind big boulders or in the darkness of deep caverns shrouded by forests and dense jungle. They were watching the night skies, in awed fascination or shrinking in fright from the hoarse rumbles and cliff-crashing reverberations preceding and accompanying the most appalling earthquake that has ever shaken and convulsed our earth. And well might they be afraid! They were undergoing the greatest disaster that has ever befallen man since he had quitted he monkey trees, straightened his back and become true man, homo sapiens. Night and day the ground shook and heaved. On the seacoasts, looking eastwards towards a great island continent, where dwelt a race of men like gods, who had evolved a high type of civilization, terrific tidal waves were rolling in higher than the highest hills. They crashed on the beaches with immense force and a momentum carrying them very far inland, while colossal league-long rollers came on behind.

Whole countrysides that had never seen the sea were drowned, while the waves, like some gigantic bore or eagre, swept up the sides of mountains and even drove backward the powerful current of deep, wide rivers. Night closed down in terror. There came a rain of fire from the heavens, which set ablaze great primeval forests, or cut mile-long swathes in them when the searing wave and blast of hot air and gases, preceding the incandescent metallic core of the immense meteorites, scorched over the woods, rolling up earth as a scroll of the past that had now no meaning or validity.

As the appalling night wore on, the terrifying noises reached a truly diabolical crescendo of crashing detonations. It seemed as if Titans in the skies were bombarding the earth with a deluge of rocks, cleaving earth's skin in order to penetrate the magma that lies deep below. The watchers began to fancy that the heavens were drawing nearer the earth, which was behaving very much like a planet that has been forced out of her orbit under great stresses and gravitational pulls from without.

THE TERROR OF THE DARKENED SUN

Came day, or a slight lessening of the nocturnal blackness, and the light of the sun appeared to have gone out like a candle blown out on an altar. For many days, indeed, night and day could hardly be told apart. A great pall of black smoke covered the vault. No light pierced the blackness, unless the vivid, eyeball-searing blaze of lightning of an electric glare never seen before even in that subtropical country, or the white flare of the sudden fall of an aerolite.

At times, when the pall of smoke showed a rent in its veil, the sun hung like a ball of blood, but the penumbra soon darkened all the air, as in time of eclipse. Then, an immense cloud of reddish powder filled the air, and to the terrified Bushmen it looked as if the whole world were now going to blaze up. The powder was followed by a rain of fine cinders, which covered the trees still left in the devastated forests and blanketed the vegetation with white.

Now the watchers and listeners cohered on the earth in the heart-sickening fear of a man who hears the shriek and whistle of a falling high-explosive bomb deepening its pitch, before it crashes near to where he lies. The air was pierced by an ear-shattering shriek, then another and another and another. Four tremendous explosions made the ground tremble. Men clinging to trees on the tops of hills were thrown to the earth. Four enormous white-hot globes had fallen from the sky into the forest behind the screen of trees. The river that flowed nearby became a cloud of hissing steam, which rose into the air of the night and increased the already terrible heat engendered by the flames, springing up from the mass of compressed air, glowing white-hot and incandescent, that is borne in front of aerolites.

Scenes like this were witnessed on a great belt all around our globe, stretching from the isles of Java and Malaysia, right across the Pacific to the Andes of South America and the high sierras of Old Mexico and the Antillean Islands of the Caribbean, on over the South and North Atlantic to the shores of North Africa and the greater Mediterranean Basin. They were seen, too, in Northern but not Central Asia.

THE LEGEND OF THE VISITING WHITE MEN

One Bushman, more daring than any other of his cowering clan, ventured out from his "air-raid" shelter into the night in a lull of the cosmic bombardment, when the pall of smoke had partly cleared, and saw, as he said, two moons riding in the sky, where before there had been no moon! Far out over the ocean, raging in a tumult never before seen by man, a whole vast island-continent in the South Atlantic had vanished, and a highly civilized people numbering in the millions, whose pioneers had contacted the Bushmen, had been swallowed up in an abyss which engulfed great palaces and temples and high towers in the depths of the sea. This is a "legend" told among the South African Bushmen even to this day!

(A note from Harold T. Wilkins: Lest the reader suppose that this is a fantasy of my invention, I may point out that the Herreros, or Ova-hereros, a turbulent Bantu people of former German South-West Africa, have an ancient tradition that after a great deluge, two white men arrived among them, as their ancestors were refuging on mountaintops. They add that these white people became the ancestors of the black Ova-hereros, which doubtless means that the strangers acted the part of apostles of a civilization from a vanished continent. The Bushmen of the Kalahari are, of course, neighbors of the Ova-hereros.

Also, the Namaqua Hottentots, in the west of Cape Colony, report the arrival of what they call a "swimming house," or Noah's Ark, very long ages ago, aboard which were men and cattle. These men settled in the country and among them was one Heitsi-Eibib, a pioneer of culture who, says an ancient tradition, "came from the east," which may or may not denote an Atlantean colony of the Old World. In the Sahara Desert are races with traditions of an appalling convulsion, which created the Sahara and also destroyed vestiges of a very ancient civilization.)

Then torrents of rain, lasting many days, forty, says the story in the Hebrew Book of Genesis, fell hissing on the hot earth. Across the raging ocean, in far-away Brazil, to the west, aboriginal Indians who had taken refuge on the summits of the Sierra do Mar, the eastern coastal range of Old Brazil, said there were great and terrible rumblings, both above and below ground. The sun and stars turned red, blue and yellow, and wild beasts mingled fearlessly with men. "A whole month passed, and our forefathers heard a roar and saw darkness ascending from the earth to the sky, while thunder rolled terrifyingly and great rain in spouts blotted out the earth and made day night. People fled to the trees for refuge against the rising waters, and many died of hunger and cold as they hung perched on the highest boughs."

THE SURVIVORS REJOICE

"Human nature was never lost, even in the days when the world perished," says an Aztec Codex, "and so the ancients celebrated their feast of the renewal of the human race."

UFOs Attack Earth ... The Out of Control Universe of Harold T. Wilkins

It is remarkable that in far-away Egypt of the Pharaohs there was in the great hall of the temple of Rameses at Karnak by the Nile, a picture with a legend of a feast of renewal celebrating and mourning the loss of a drowned continent in the Western Ocean. In those days of the pyramids, it cannot be suggested that ancient Mexicans cut or painted such a picture on the walls or pillars of the temple of ancient Karnak, more than 6,400 miles away.

The ancient Mexicans recorded three great catastrophes, of which the third was the supreme disaster. They were caused, say their traditions, by volcanic fires, tidal waters, and hurricanes. They participated together, say the ancient Mexican traditions, in shaking the earth at various times. Each catastrophe was followed by an era of ruin, and the destruction of the human race. Men climbed trees, ran everywhere in their terror, crowding and pushing together, embarked in ships, hid themselves in caves, got on mountaintops. The few survivors were so far dispersed that they thought they were alone in the world. Every four years, a fiesta was held in Central America, wherein ancient princes and peoples prostrated themselves before the gods, praying for no return of these calamities. Dances and feasts celebrated the escape of the survivors.

UFOs Attack Earth . . . The Out of Control Universe of Harold T. Wilkins

A Ghostly Underground World

In *Mysteries of Ancient South America*, Harold T. Wilkins explores the always-interesting topic of hidden tunnels and labyrinths. In this case, Wilkins recounts stories of tunnels first dug by the Atlanteans and then later co-opted by the native races that came to take their place. The stories of the various subterranean civilizations include Amazon woman defending themselves from rapists who also practiced cannibalism, as well as tales of a hidden paradise called Agharti, lit by a strange, life-enhancing green glow and ruled over by kindly kings.

TUNNELING TO PARDISE

Tunnels and labyrinths have played a mysterious part in ancient civilizations in regions that may wrongly be called the older worlds of Asia and Europe and Africa. Who can say what the ancient priest-emperors of old Peru knew of, or had inherited, from these vanished civilizations, which are not even a name, or more than a faint and ghostly shadow? An ancient tradition of the Brahmanic Hindostan speaks of a large island of "unparalleled beauty" which, in very ancient times, lay in the middle of a vast sea in Central Asia, north of what is now the Himalayas. A race of nephilim, or men of a golden age, lived in the island, but there was no communication between them and the mainland, except through tunnels, radiating in all directions, and many hundreds of miles long.

Among the Mongolian tribes of Inner Mongolia, even today, there are traditions about tunnels and subterranean worlds, which sound as fantastic as anything in modern novels. One legend, if it be that, says that the tunnels lead to a subterranean world of Antediluvian descent somewhere in a recess of Afghanistan, or in the region of the Hindu Kush. It is a Shangri-la, where science and the arts, never threatened by world wars, develop peacefully, among a race of vast knowledge. It is even given a name: Agharti. The legend adds that a labyrinth of tunnels and underground passages is extended in a series of links connection Agharti with all other such subterranean worlds!

Tibetan lamas even assert that in America—it is not stated whether North, Central or South—there live in vast caves of an underworld, reached by secret tunnels, peoples of an ancient world who thus escaped a tremendous cataclysm of thousands of years ago. Both in Asia and America, these fantastic and ancient races are alleged to be governed by benevolent rulers, or King-Archons. The subterranean world, it is said, is lit by a strange green luminescence, which favors the growth of crops and conduces to length of days and health.

Ferdinand Ossendowski, in his book **Beasts, Men and Gods**, also mentions this strange Kingdom of Agharti, which, he says, he has been told by learned Chinese lamas and Mongolian princes, has many men and tribes of incredibly ancient races, long vanished from the kingdoms of today. He mentions an old Brahman of Nepal who, on a mystic pilgrimage, met a fisherman, apparently in the interior or on the coast of Siam, or Thailand, or maybe another part of Indo-China, who ordered the Brahman to take a place in a boat, obey the will of the gods by sailing with him on the sea to an Arabian Nights island where live people "having two tongues" which "can separately speak different languages." He landed in the mysterious island, which Monsieur Ossendwoski does not say might very well be located somewhere in the rock-pinnacle and coral-studded China Sea, a region shunned and unexplored today, off the main stream lanes, and not even charted by the Admiralty, who advise navigators to stick to the well-known sea lanes. But wherever it might be, these strange islanders showed the old lama a bird with teeth that caught sea fish and an unknown animal with sixteen feet and one eye. The islanders said, "We come out of the subterranean kingdom, where, in cars of type unknown to Western races, men rush through the subterranean world through cleavages in the earth."

Clearly, this story is of the believe-it-or-not type; but it would be wisdom not to dismiss the story as pure fantasy. There is no smoke without fire, nor all the Eastern wandering mystics necessarily romancers of the Baron von Munchausen type, nor men whose imaginations have been over-strongly impressed by the fantasy and most entertaining novels of the H.G. Wells of a more youthful day! I say gently, again, reader, remember the Komodo dragon; and I could also add, of my own curious knowledge, the strange parchment charts of the China Sea of the year 1669, kept by Captain William Kidd, the pirate-privateer, whose originals are now in a house in Essex.

THE EMBITTERED PERUVIAN

For what purposes, however, were these amazingly long tunnels of old Peru intended? What mysterious cults did they serve?

A startling clue, gained in a very peculiar and romantic manner, to one of the purposes of these mysterious tunnels, and which is directly concerned with the mysterious stone city of in the Lancandones territory, of which I have written elsewhere, came in the course of a chance talk between a very old Peruvian—a Quicha Indian—and the well-known mystic and American woman traveler, the late Madame Helena P. Blavatskaya, who, as one sees, was journeying through the mountains of Peru in 1851 or 1853. The old Peruvian had passed all his life vainly trying to conceal his hatred towards the official Peruvians and the Spanish conquerors. He called them brigands.

"I keep friends with them, these bandidos," he said, "and their Catholic missionaries, for the sake of my own people. But I am as much a worshipper of the sun as if I had lived in the days of our murdered emperor, the Inca Atahualpha. Now, as a converted native and missionary, I once took a journey to Santa Cruz del Quich (in Western Guatemala), and, when there, I went to see some of my people by a subterranean passage leading into a mysterious city behind the cordilleras. Herein, it is death for any white man to trespass!"

Said Madame Blavatskaya, "We believe his story. Besides, a man who is about to die will rarely stop to invent idle stories."

Similar strange tunnels of incredibly ancient date, and unknown origin, in the West Indies, were brought to the attention of Christopher Columbus, when he visited Martinique. No doubt, the white, Atlantean race built splendid cities in what are now West Indian islands, but which, at the far-off date, may have formed part of a now submerged middle American continent, whose name is commemorated in the word "Antilles."

UFOs Attack Earth ... The Out of Control Universe of Harold T. Wilkins

THE CANNIBAL RAPISTS OF MARTINIQUE

A curious tradition of the old world of Asia is that old Atlantis had a network of labyrinthine tunnels and passages running in all directions, in the day when the land-bridge between the drowned land and Africa, on one side, and old Brazil, on the other, still existed. In Atlantis, the tunnels were used for necromantic and black magic cults. Anyway, it is curious that the Caribs, in 1493, told Columbus that, in the old kingdom of the Amazon, women warriors, anciently existing in Mandanino, or Martinique, there were great subterraneans, and when the women were likely to be pestered, out of due season of love, orgasm and rutting, by periodical, cannibal lovers, the women went down to the great tunnels and hid themselves. If the lovers, not to be put off, still followed them, their ardent passions were cooled with showers of well-aimed arrows from Amazon bows, and many a cannibal beau was brought to an untimely grave in this way by the fierce Venuses of old Martinique.

Queer caverns were also among the discoveries of the conquistadors in Hispaniola, or San Domingo. One of them, named "Jouanabaina," was on the land of the canique of Machinech, and the object of the worship of the natives. It was ornamented with various paintings. They are natural excavations lit from the top, so as to let pass the first rays of the rising sun. The interior of these grottos is covered with idols, carved, engraved and inlaid in the rock, in rude and bizarre forms—toads with heads at the end of their feet, monstrous human figures with crooked bodies diminishing like a cone, terminated by a spherical knob, tortoises, and other animals, especially snakes.

THE MINGLING OF THE ATLANTEAN RACES

In Haiti, there are remains of a people of unknown race and date who knew not of iron. Like the race in Atlantean Brazil, they seem to have been heliolithic, and of very advanced culture. The statues show that two races existed there thousands of years ago: one white, the other black. One of the heads is a sculpted funerary face of a white man, and another of a white woman of Atlantean type. There is also a remarkable head of a black woman, in polished but weathered granite of prehistoric date, which bears a strange resemblance to in shape and peculiar coronal headdress to a splendid terra-cotta head of a Negro

Venus, found in British Nigeria and now in the palace of the native ruler of Ife, where it is worshipped as a goddess. (As doubtless was this similar head in Atlantean old Haiti.) The Nigerian head of great beauty was carved by an artist of great skill belonging to a very ancient, advanced, black civilization in Africa.

Frobenius, who associated this ancient culture of West Africa with Atlantis, was probably right. Had he seen this similar head in Haiti, he would also have remembered that, in Atlantis and her colonies and empire, red, white and black races commingled. Part of the old Empire of Atlantis extended from the far greater Gulf of Maranon—the Gulf of Mexico today—into the island-continent as it was the West Indies, not then shattered by cataclysm.

One may also infer from these pictures that, in pre-Columbian Haiti, that necromancy and black magic of the Voodoo type existed in this strange island long ages before either the Spanish or French introduced Negro slaves into old Hispaniola. Who can say whether such black cults came there from the motherland of Atlantis far gone in decay?

There are also extremely ancient petroglyphs of a curiously symbolic whorled type recalling similar inscriptions in modern Colombia both baffling to modern archeologists and pre-historians. Yes, on Haiti-Dominica, too, rests the shadow of Great Atlantis!

UFOs Attack Earth . . . The Out of Control Universe of Harold T. Wilkins

UFOs Attack Earth... The Out of Control Universe of Harold T. Wilkins

Strange Creatures and Monsters Galore

One of the most fascinating phases in the career of Harold T. Wilkins came in the latter part of the 1940s when he produced an intriguing monograph called *Monsters and Mysteries of America, the Jungles, the Tropics, and the Arctic Wastes.* The subtitle of this rather condensed—and certainly straightforward—tome is *Strange Stories of Modern Adventures Suggesting That The King Kongs And The Dinosaurs May Still Be Alive Today.* Not only is that a whopper of a title—even longer than the one given to this contemporary edition showcasing his literary skills—but it makes by far the most exaggerated claims to be found in any of Wilkins' work. It appears as we flip through the pages that Wilkins has donned a professor's cap and a detective's spyglass, a la Indiana Jones, and has taken to the rugged back roads and dense jungles twisted with impenetrable vines in search of beasts long thought to have dissolved into time.

TALL TALES VERSUS SCIENTIFIC SKEPTICISM

It is possible that in remote and still unexplored regions of the earth, in the depths of the seas and far-ranging oceans, monsters and strange forms of life exist which are unknown to, and therefore unclassified, by scientists and natural historians, or oceanographical museum experts?

Palaeontologists are apt to smile at such a question as being absurd. They will point out that such phenomena as the ice ages, or the glaciation of the climate over thousands of years—which north and south of the equator, followed life's long summer on earth, when gigantic saurians wallowed in the slime of the warm beaches of shallower seas and dinosaurs ranged a much lower land—exterminated all such genera and species. Marine biologists, too, usually scout the idea that there may still exist in the great depths of the oceans, or in the mid-deeps, any such monsters as "sea serpents." They ask us to name any oceanographical museum or marine biological institute of research which possesses a bone of such creatures.

However, in this latter connection, I happen to possess photographs of monstrous-shaped and sized skulls and vertebrae in private collections. I can quote from the logs of a modern British warship, and the journal of a German submarine commander in the First World War, who, after torpedoing and watching the sinking, in the mid-Atlantic, of a British freighter, witnessed the throwing up from the depths a monstrous sea saurian unknown to marine biology. This should warn against dogmatism on such matters. It is also a fact that more of these events might be entered in the logs of British warships were it not for the fact that their lordships of the British Board of Admiralty are apt to cast a malign eye on the prospects of promotion of any officer who enters such an event in his log or journal.

On land, the wild animal trapper, out "to bring 'em back alive" from the jungles and bush of Africa or Asia says, with a skeptical smile, that it is not unknown for Negroes in regions remote from the confines of civilization to tell stories of strange animals and fearsome monsters in lone and unexplored forests and jungles which have never been seen by a white man. The trapper adds that if he were to let such stories divert him from the main trail of his safari, he would never bring anything back alive—save a reputation for naïve credulity, which would prejudice him in the eyes of directors of zoological parks, or wild animal dealers.

PLATEAUX OF WESTERN U.S. AND "LOST WORLD" OF BRAZIL

And yet, before we dismiss all such stories to the limbo of travelers' tales—and the "anthropophagi and men whose heads do hang beneath their shoulders"—we must bear in mind that, in old Asia, and even older North and South America, there are vast areas which have never been under sea since the Eocene Age. One of them is the 1,500,000 square mile region, still unexplored, of the Roosevelt-Govaz tableland, in central Brazil. Another is the high plateaux section of Nevada, Arizona, Colorado and Utah. This latter arid and alkaline territory is said to be one of the oldest parts of the world above sea level. The central Brazilian tableland of mysteries, bounded by the Rio Araguaya, tributary of the mighty Amazon, or Maranon, and intersected by the mostly unexplored Rios Xingu and Tapajos, (latitude 5 degrees S. to 12 degrees S., and longitude 50 degrees to 63 degrees W.) is characterized by plutonic rocks and a queer plant louse. The rocks have been formed under the influence of volcanic fires, and there are no alluvial layers denoting past submersion. The louse, called "Brazilaphis Bondari," after the Brazilian professor Bondar, of Russian origin, lives on the lowest parts of plants and any inundation would at once have exterminated this most ancient insect as it has in other parts of the world. Taken together, the two facts suggest that this strange region of Brazil and its Asiatic counterpart of Angara, in the Siberian provinces of Irkutsk and Yakutsk, where similar phenomena have been observed, may never have been under water since the azoic age.

Even the most conservative geologists who have visited the central Brazilian tableland admit that it has been above sea level for a much earlier epoch than the last glacial age.

I have mentioned this Brazilian "Lost World" at some length because the Indians of the Matto Grosso of Brazil, which lies near it, say that it has a vast belt of rivers, swamps and marshy jungles and forests, which date back to the far day of the rising of the Andes. They say that great lizards of the type of the prehistoric saurian, extinct elsewhere on the earth millions of years ago, still wallow in its swamps and emerge on the beaches of great lagoons. Later, I shall tell a story which purports that a great ape of a veritable "King Kong" type is among the fearsome inhabitants of this lost world, which was, say forest Indian traditions, the home of a white and highly civilized race who thousands of years ago ruled the Indians' ancestors.

J. LERIUS MEETS MONSTER LIZARD ON ISLAND NEAR RIO

One of the earliest stories of an encounter with an unknown monster in the Americas occurs in the account of the travels of Jean Lerius, a Frenchman. He was one of the company of Admiral Nicolas Durand de Villegagnon, who, in 1555, attempted to found a French colony, called "Nouvelle Geneve" (New Geneva), in an island in the bay of Rio de Janeiro. It was about the year 1557, when Lerius and two other Frenchmen, who had no "hand gunnes," but "only our swords," were in a wood in the interior of Brazil.

"We had not Barbarians (Indians) to guide us, and therefore wandered in the woods and passed through a deep valley, hearing the noise of a certain beast coming towards us, supposing it to be some timorous and harmless wild beast, notwithstanding, proceeding on our intended journey, we were secure and quiet in our mind, but presently, thirty paces distant from us, on the right hand, we saw a lizard on a hill, bigger than the body of a man, and five or six feet long. He, being spread all over with white and rough scales like oyster shells, holding up one of his forefeet, with his head aloft, and staring eyes began to behold us.

"Wherefore, being astonished (for none of us, as it then fell out, carried a hand gunne, but had only our swords at our sides, and bows and arrows, which weapons could not greatly hurt that Monster, armed with such hard scales). Notwithstanding, fearing lest if we shifted ourselves by flight, being swifter than we, he would dispatch us altogether. The one fearfully beheld the other, and we stood still in the same place. But after that prodigious, fearful lizard had beheld us a quarter of an hour, with an open mouth, and because it was exceeding hot weather (for it was a clear day, almost at noon), fetching a deep groan, that we might easily hear it, upon a sudden, he went unto the top of a mountain, with so great noise of the crashing and breaking of twigs and boughs, as of a deer running through a wood which could scarce have made more noise, we, therefore, who were then much affrighted not being very careful to pursue him, gave thanks to God and pursued our intended journey. And embracing their opinion, who affirm that the lizard is delighted with the sight of man, it seemed to me that the beholding of us pleased the Monster so much as we were tormented through his presence."

This adventure occurred in the country of the Tupinambas Indians. The description of Lerius does not fit the structure of the cayman, or any alligator or crocodile known to zoology, and however it may be with the quaint notion of Lerius that the monster was pleased with the sight of men, the story suggests that there was as much fear on one side as there was anything but delight on the other. It was probably lucky for the Frenchmen that they had no "hand gunnes"; for the use of such primitive matchlocks of those days would doubtless have led to the death of some of the men. In days far later than those of Lerius, roamers in the jungles of South America have found it wiser to forbear the use of weapons when suddenly encountering wild beasts, whose reaction from fear of man to fury is apt to be both sudden and fatal to the men!

UNICORNS IN THE U.S.A.?

Our next story of an alleged encounter with a strange animal—this time, in North America—is of the believe-it-or-not sort. The monster concerned seems akin to one of those who, today, figures in the coat of arms painted on the state motorcars of King George of Buckingham Palace and Windsor Castle, England. Nevertheless, the skeptic often has a soft spot in his heart for a mystery, whether or no his intellect and powers of rationality permit him to accept such stories at their face value.

An English sailor, named David Ingram, traveled in 1568-69 from the "Rios das Minas on the Gulf of Mexico," to Cape Breton, in Accadia, or modern Nova Scotia. The story of his travels, which was an exceedingly daring trip in days when little or nothing was known of the vast stretch of territory from Florida up to what is now Maine and Nova Scotia, occurs in an exceedingly rare "Relacion," no copy of which exists in the British museum, and whose reprint in a rare book of Colonel Charles Jennett Weston, of Carolina, in 1856, would be reckoned a rare capture by a wealthy bibliophile of today.

Ingram had two other sailor pals with him and the men seem to have been castaways from some wreck off the coast of Mexico. He entered an elusive country called Norimbega, found mapped only in rare and ornamental atlases of the spouting dolphin and Princess Pocahontas vintage of the late 16th and early 17th centuries. The name seems to be a garbling of Norway, and in Andre Thevet's "Cosmographie," published in Paris, in 1575, Norimbega is located about the region covered by Massachusetts, Vermont, Maine and New Hampshire.

Says Ingram: "Our expedition did also see in those countries a Monstrous Beast, twice as big as a horse and in every proportion like unto a horse, both in mane and hooves, hair and neighing, save that it was small towards the hind parts like a greyhound. These Beasts have two teeth or horns of a foot long growing straight forth out of their nostrils. They are natural enemies of the horse. I did also see in that country both elephants and panthers, and one other strange beast bigger than a bear; yet it had neither head nor neck, and his eyes and mouth were in his breast; this beast is very ugly to behold, and cowardly of kind, yet bears a very fine skin like a rat, full of silver hair."

THE RED MEN LIKE THEIRS ROASTED

About 150 years later, a French explorer, Monsieur Benard de la Harpe, writing in 1719, says he found animals like those mentioned by Ingram—meaning, apparently, Unicorns!—in the country round the middle course of the Red River of Louisiana. La Harpe's expedition joined a party of Nawidishe Indians, near the confluence of the Washita and Red Rivers, then known as the False Washita, of the Indian Territory. He says that these Indians were then engaged in "roasting unicorns." La Harpe describes these beasts as about the size of a common horse, with reddish hair as long as the hair of a goat, thin legs, and single horn six inches long in the middle of the forehead. The horn did not branch out into prongs or tines. The meat was palatable.

He adds: "This description agrees well with what Monsieur de Bienville heard from the savages upon the upper Washita River, that unicorns were there to be found."

It may be noted that this usually considered fabulous animal was said by Pliny and Aristotle to be a one-horned beast as large as a horse. Also, the description does not fit that of a buffalo, or the American bison, which then, as we know, roamed the prairies.

Dinosaurs Haunt America

Marching through the foliage of time, we continue to excerpt from Wilkins' pint-sized monograph, which was originally published as one of the immensely popular, twenty-five cent "little-big books," advertised in *The Police Gazette* and the comic books of the day. *Monsters and Mysteries of America, the Jungles, the Tropics and the Arctic Wastes* contains fascinating accounts of strange felines terrorizing America in the 1700s. Wilkins next moves on to reports of dinosaurs seen in North America, offering up the radical perspective that perhaps man and the dinosaurs shared the Earth and were not widely separated in time, as most scientists would insist, even today. These same dinosaurs might be known to eat the odd American Indian now and then, as one story declares.

JEFFERSON REPORTS ON FOSSIL OF PRE-HISTORIC FELINE

Now we may pass on to a remarkable story of an adventure of a hunter in Virginia who encountered a strange monster "whose roarings shook the ground, and which carried off horses as if they were sheep." (These were the words of President Jefferson.) In the American Philosophical Society's transactions of 1799, Jefferson reported that laborers, digging a cave at Greenbriar, in western Virginia, unearthed at a depth of three feet the bones of an unknown species of clawed animal. The earth was "nitrous," and the bones were those of an unguiculated (nailed or clawed) quadruped, "the lion being his nearest neighbor in size." But the monster, on the evidence of the remains in the case, must have been three times the size of a lion, or *Leo Africanus*.

"MEGALONYX" OF JEFFERSON ENCOUNTERED IN THE FLESH

At this date, there existed traditions that the early adventurers in the county of Greenbriar, Virginia, were alarmed at their first camp, in the night of their arrival, by the terrible roarings of some beast unknown to them. He went round and round their camp, and they saw his eyes shining like two balls of fire. So terrified were their horses, that they crouched down, trembling and sweating on the ground, while their hunting dogs crept in among them, not daring even to bark. Their campfires, it was thought, protected them; but next morning the would-be settlers packed up and quitted the country as too dangerous for men to live in, in isolated cabins.

This encounter happened about the year 1760. In 1765, two men, George Wilson and John Davies, went on a hunting trip to the Cheat River, a branch of the Monongahela, in western Virginia. One night, some way from their camp, they heard coming a tremendous roar which became louder, till it seemed like thunder, and the ground seemed to be all of a tremble with the reverberations. Whatever this animal was, it remained near their camp for a long time and appeared to be prowling around. Their dogs, normally savage animals, crept to the men's feet and would not budge an inch from the fire. They would neither quit the camp nor bark.

In a few moments, the hunters heard an answering roar from the top of a mountain about a mile off, and in a minute or two came a roar from a neighboring knob of the mountain. A Colonel John Stewart had this story from Wilson when he met him, in 1769. In the Revolutionary War, Stewart was colonel of the regiment in which Wilson was a private. He also heard the same story from Davies, who, in 1799, was living down in "ole Kaintuck." And truly, even the boys of "old Kaintuck" might have sheered off any close encounter with this monster, whom President Jefferson styled the "megalonyx."

In South Africa, so Jefferson was told, dogs behaved in the same way when large, man-eating lions were around.

Another man named Draper came to close quarters with this mysterious "megalonyx" when he was hunting along the Kanhawa in 1790. Draper turned his horse loose to graze, with a bell on his neck. Hardly had the horse got clear of a belt of wood, still within earshot, when the bell began to ring furiously and rapidly. Draper, grabbing his rifle, turned back, thinking that hostile Indians were around, but before he arrived on the spot where the bell was ringing, the horse had been half eaten up. Draper's dog, scenting the trail of a wild beast, followed hard on the scent and presently came in sight of an animal of enormous size. Draper, who was close behind the dog, was a daring hunter and crack shot, but he was so dumbfounded at the sight of so fearsome a beast, that he at once withdrew from sight and as silently as possible checked and brought off his dog. He said, afterwards, that he could recall no more of the monster than his enormous size, and that his general outlines were of the feline type. It was certainly not a panther or any animal known to him.

OLD WORLD PETROGLYPHS IN CAVE

That huge and unknown animals have existed in the far past in North America—which probably better deserves the title of *old world*, in both an ethnological and a zoological sense than Europe does—is suggested by a remarkable discovery made in a cave in Ohio, about 1810, at a location some 20 miles below the mouth of the Wabash. The cave is in a big rock which stands just above the water when the river is in flood. In the days of the early settlers of Ohio, the cave was a rendezvous of ruffians, robbers and high-jackers hailing from Kentucky. These outlaws terrorized all traffic up and down the river. They ravaged, plundered, and murdered over a wide territory. The gang was led by a fellow named Wilson.

Here is an account given by a little known American writer of the early 1820s:

"Wilson brought his family to the cave and fitted it up as a dwelling. He put out a sign on a board on the waterside: 'Wilson's Liquor Vault and House of Entertainment.' He organized a band of robbers and formed plans to murder crews of boats who stopped at his tavern. Then he manned the boats with his own thugs and sent them to New Orleans, where their lading was sold. The cash was conveyed by hand through the states of Tennessee and Kentucky, and on the road, the returning party were ordered to ambush and rob and murder likely men. Presently, the robbed merchants and relatives of good and respectable men, who had gone missing and were never heard of again, offered rewards. It was found that Wilson, at the head of 35 thugs, had a hide-out and observation post at Hurricane Island, where every passing boat was stopped and looted.

"He had fences and receivers at Natchez and New Orleans, and the cave was his treasure vault. The cave was entered after the Wilson gang had been rounded up. It was found to be 12 rods long and five wide, but what excited astonishment was that the cave proved to be the home, or religious center, of some ancient and unknown race. The floor was as flat as the pavement of an old cathedral in England and the sides rose in stony grades like the seats in a theater pit. On the walls had been executed glyphs of unknown animals.

"Beyond and above the cavern lay another even more gloomy cave. It was joined to it by a passage or an opening of around 14 feet, to ascend which was like passing up a chimney. Far above was the mountain. Some time after the robbers had been broken up, searchers in the upper cavern found six skeletons, but it cannot be said whether they were prehistoric or the remains of men murdered by Wilson and his gang."

On the walls of the lower cave—besides curious glyphs of the phases of the sun and moon, a panther held by his ears by a child, a buzzard tearing out the heart of a prostrate man, a crocodile, scorpions, and a curious hydra serpent—were no fewer than eight images of animals of unknown type. Three of these looked like elephants without tusks or tails, one like a toxodon, another like a tiger, and the last like a quadrumane whose claws were alike before and behind. This strange monster was depicted as in the act of conveying something to its mouth, which was located in its middle.

In passing, one may add, though it has no immediate concern with the subject of this booklet, that the cave walls bore fine and striking images of ancient clothed men and woman, by no means like Amero-Indians, but wearing rich cloaks, breeches open at the knees, sandals tied across the toes and heels, a bandeau tied with feathers encircling the head. The dress of the women resembled that of classic Greece, the hair clasped with a crown confined by a bodkin, and they had a sort of stola or gown, and a zone or cestus confining an "indusium," or female undergarment; they also were sandaled. Finally, there was a curious glyph of a serpent biting its tail, in an orb or circle, which, in the ancient world, symbolized the rotation of the earth and the planets, and the notion that matter and the world were renewed by feeding on themselves.

It is possible that this strange race were coeval with the dead cities of old Brazil, referred to above. Neither Wilson nor any member of his gang of robbers had the knowledge necessary to have faked such remarkable petroglyphs, nor any inducement or inclination to carry out such works, requiring artistic skill and a considerable degree of classic culture. In that, they resembled the old *bandeiristas* (land pirates) of Brazil who, in 1750, blundered on the ruins of a dead and extremely ancient city in the interior of Bahia province, located on the ancient Highlands of old Brazil.

A REPTILE "MOSQUETO" NEAR SYRACUSE; A HORNED SERPENT WHOSE STENCH COULD KILL

The North American Indians, from the shores of Florida, right up into the Arctic Circle, have folklore and traditions about the past existence of monsters, which are not always mere fables and fairytales of the childhood of the race.

David Cusick, in a rare pamphlet on the "History of the Six Indian Nations," published at Lewiston, N.Y., in 1828, collected from the Oneida branch of the Tuscaroras a story about a great reptile called the "Mesqueto," which invaded their ancient lands from Lake Onondaga and killed a number of people. Authentic or not, up until about 1885, tracks of some queer birdlike monster—about 20 inches long and extending for 20 rods—were to be seen near Brighton, south of Syracuse, N.Y., though it is rather suspiciously added that the Indians often renewed the track of this monster. They also have stories about a great horned serpent that appeared in Lake Ontario, "2,200 years before the time of Columbus," whose stench killed many people. This was about the time when a "blazing star," or immense aerolite fell into an Indian fort on the St. Lawrence and actually did kill off a number of the red men.

WAS EARLY MAN COEVAL WITH DINOSAURS?

Dinosaurs of the Mesozoic Age do not seem to have left a trace of themselves in America's Tertiary rocks, says Dr. R.S. Lull, professor of vertebrate paleontology, at Yale University, in 1917. He says that the rising of the land and the draining of the great inland Cretaceous seas along the low-lying shores, where the dinosaurs had their home, spelled their doom. But the career of these immense reptilia of geologic ages was *not* brief. In fact, it seems to have lasted for an evolutionary period three times as long as that of the entire mammalian age. The dinosaur does not represent a futile attempt on the part of Nature to people the earth with creatures of insignificant moment. These monsters are comparable in their majestic rise, slow culmination, and dramatic fall to the greatest nations of antiquity. So says the professor.

Yet, there have been recent discoveries in U.S. territory which suggest that early man, contrary to the accepted theories of the paleontologists and evolutionists, may have been coeval with dinosaurs who managed to survive cataclysmic upheavals in other parts of the earth. Let us glance at this evidence.

A DINOSAUR IDOL FOUND AT GRANBY, CALIFORNIA

In 1926, a man named Jordan was digging to make a garage at a place near Granby, California. He uncovered a queer idol at a depth of 12 feet. I have a sketch of it. There were other remains that suggested that an ancient settlement had once existed nearby. But the idol was of a hard green stone like nothing known in the locality. It may have come from a long distance, for it suggests the Amazon stone or chalcuhitl, well known in ancient Mexico. It is found, even today, among the Brazilian Indians along the Rio Tapajos, where it is called the baraquita or muyrakyta and is, or used to be made from a green clay, found under water and hardening on exposure to air.

On this hard, green stone idol, carved in high relief, is the figure of a dinosaur and what looks like an elephant with a long curved trunk.

A DINOSAUR MUMMY DISCOVERED IN "BAD LANDS" OF WYOMING

In the Bad Lands of Wyoming, Charles Sternberg found a dinosaur mummy of the Trochodont, or duck-billed dinosaur. He describes this find and shows a picture of it in his book, ***The Life of a Fossil Hunter***. The American Museum of New York acquired this queer mummy, which exhibits dried-up flesh and skin texture.

This raises a query: if dinosaurs became extinct 12 million years ago, how could this mummy have lasted that period, under any conditions, without turning to dust? It must be remembered that it was exposed to weather—rain, snow, frost and the heat of summer. The only answer that can be advanced to this riddle is, as has been suggested: While dinosaurs died out, millions of years ago, in the so-called older worlds of Europe and Asia, something favored their survival, in America, to the age of early man, who may have lived at a period in the Tertiary, and not merely in the later Quaternary age, as evolutionists have previously supposed. Indeed, as the years go by in this century, not only may the archeology of North and South America have to be revised in relation to the immense antiquity of civilized men, but also the paleontology and geology in relation to other forms of life. Science has no room for dogmas, which it can well afford to leave to the established religions and superstitions, which batten on the closing of ears and the calcification of brains at the command of "infallible" pontiffs.

DINOSAUR TRACKS FOUND NEAR PAINTED DESERT

It has been said that the dinosaurs throve in an atmosphere of carbonic acid gas, and that the dense flora of the Mesozoic Ages absorbed the carbon and released oxygen, thereby making for conditions suitable to mammals. But if the age of dinosaurs lasted for the immense period for which Professor Lull contends, then some form of dinosaurs may have adjusted themselves to changing conditions, and aquatic and land dinosaurs may have existed in America long after man appeared. It is a curious fact that tracks of dinosaurs have recently been found in stone on the edges of the Painted Desert of Arizona.

MONSTER-SCARED INDIANS LIVE
IN LAKE HOUSES, FORTS

It is also curious that traditions of the Indian Six Nations purport that, thousands of years ago, their ancestors were attacked by some type of dinosaur that came out of the waters of Lake Erie, in the night, devoured some of the people, and forced the rest to abandon their villages and retreat to the shelter of their stockaded forts. In another case, in Canada, the Indians say that, anciently, men built dwellings on stakes in lakes, like the lake dwellings in Switzerland, in order to escape monsters who were ravaging the country, though what are implied seem to be mammoths.

UFOs Attack Earth . . . The Out of Control Universe of Harold T. Wilkins

More American Dinosaurs

In this next chapter taken from Harold T. Wilkins' 1947 booklet, there is more discussion of the idea that man and dinosaur may have once shared the same world. But even more exciting is the story of the members of an expedition to the Yukon Territory who encountered a terrifying meat-eating monster still very much alive and devastating to behold. Their hair-raising trek in the frozen tundra of the north must be read in detail to be appreciated, and the entire text of the story is reprinted here!

PICTOGRAPHS OF TYRANNOSAURUS UNEARTHED IN ARIZONA

In the Supai canon of Arizona, an American expedition, numbering California scientists among its personnel, discovered, in 1924, remarkable pictographs of unknown and extremely ancient origin, which had been cut through the iron scale on red sandstone, and which depict the most dreadful of all the dinosaurs: the terrible tyrannosaurus. This dinosaur is usually said to have been the last of the carnivorous dinosaurs, to have walked on his hind legs, and to have leapt like a kangaroo. Not the sort of beast a fossil-hunter would like to have around while he was pecking fossils, or hacking rocks in a wild gorge! Tyrannosaurus reached all of 35 feet, and is, so far, the largest known of the dinosaurs. Careful examination of the rocks disclosed the genuine antiquity of this petroglyph.

Questioned by the scientists of the expedition, the Indians of the region said the petroglyph was not done by any ancestors of theirs, but by "giant men in the long, long ago." It is certainly no joke or fake of modern origin. It shows the dinosaur erect on his hind legs with his tail extended, as the artist must have seen him, untold ages ago.

ARTIFACT OF ARMOURED STEGOSAURUS TYPE FOUND EAST OF PORTLAND, OREGON

I myself possess a photograph of an ancient carved image, found in volcanic tufa, and made by some ancient man of race unknown who once lived near the gorge of the Columbia River in Oregon. This artifact depicts a type of armored dinosaur like the stegosaurus. It is skillfully carved, is undeniably ancient, and not of Red Indian origin. The location of the find was about 15 miles east of Portland, Oregon, on the site of a later old Indian camping ground. The monster shows a formidable array of teeth, has serrated ridge armor along the top of the back, and heavy body armor. The armored legs seem to be missing.

TALL TALES FROM THE YUKON TERRITORY

All this leads us by way of preface to certain queer stories told by trappers in northern British Columbia, gold prospectors and old sourdoughs in the Yukon territory of Canada's Northwest, and Uncle Sam's Alaska.

As long ago as 1887, an American engineer from Washington, D.C., Mr. H. von Beyer, was staying at Port Townsend, Puget Sound, Washington territory, when a mysterious rumor spread around about a monstrous animal seen in the interior of Alaska. The story had probably reached Puget Sound from some trading steamship arrived from Sitka. White folk at Port Townsend told von Beyer that Indians had gone into Alaska and had taken the trail up the Yukon River. At a point a great way up into the interior, the Indians had seen strange tracks on the ground. They followed this spoor for many miles and finally came in sight of strange hairy animals of immense size and unknown species. The Indians were scared at the enormous girth of these animals, whose tracks were described as following a circular route. The story had passed through many mouths and von Beyer doubted it. He suspicioned it had come from some Vancouver Island Indians who had taken a long journey north by sea.

It may be here noted that the Iroquois Indians of New York State and of eastern Canada have old traditions of about a huge animal that traveled in circles in days long before white men discovered Canada. It had been supposed that the traditions referred to the American bison or buffalo.

However, in 1905, another and remarkable story appeared in the scientific journal published in Paris, France. It purported to relate the adventures of one George Dupuy, a French traveler, a banker of San Francisco, a French-Canadian mission priest, and an American gold-hunter and fossicker a an Indian village called Armstrong Creek, located near the McQuesten River, in the Yukon territory. This river flows through marshy tundras and alongside hills located between the 138 and 136 meridians, some 100 miles east of Dawson City as the crow flies. Here, in the neighborhood of Partridge Creek, the party encountered a terrible monster that seems to have been an Arctic dinosaur.

One Buttler, an American, and another prospector were one day hunting three large moose at the mouth of Clear Creek when, on a sudden, as they were stalking the moose down wind, they say a huge bull moose raise his head from the moss and lichens where he had been quietly browsing and give three bounds. Another moose uttered a loud bellow—given only when a mortal enemy is near, or when the moose is badly wounded—and the three moose set off at a frantic gallop to the south.

The men cautiously approached the spot, which was partly screened by pines and undergrowth, when they saw in the snow the imprint of the body of some monstrous animal whose belly had left in the slime of a river creek an impression two feet deep, 30 feet long and 12 feet wide! Four gigantic paws, deeply impressed in the muck, had left prints five feet long and two-and-a-half feet wide. There were also prints of sharp claws which measured one foot long, and were deeply embedded in the mud. The men measured the impression of a tail 10 feet long and 16 inches wide at the middle!

They trailed the monster's tracks up a valley until, after abut six miles, they entered a ravine called Partridge Creek. Here, the tracks abruptly and unaccountably ended. It looked as if the monster had given a tremendous bound up the cliff of the ravine. Deciding that the location was unhealthy, the men made tracks for an outpost.

UFOs Attack Earth... The Out of Control Universe of Harold T. Wilkins

Dupuy, when he was told the story, laughed and joked at Buttler.

Buttler angrily retorted that he and his pal were more sober than most judges when they trailed that monster's tracks. It was arranged that Buttler should guide Dupuy, the French priest, Padre Pierre Lavagneux, a Yukon sourdough, and half a dozen Indians to the spot, and for a whole day the party searched the banks of the McQuesten, the flats of Partridge Creek, and the whole countryside between the little township of Barlow, on the embouchure of the McQuesten River with the Stewart River which flows into the Yukon, and a lofty snow-covered range which numbers Mt. Haldane among its most valiant peaks.

They found nothing unusual and they reported the facts to a sergeant of the Royal Canadian Mounted Police who, though skeptical and humorous, agreed to join them in the hunt for the monster.

One evening, tired out after wading through sloughs and frozen tundras, they pulled up near the summit of a rock gulch and lit a campfire, as evening was coming on. The pine logs blazed brightly and there was the pleasant odor of turpentine and balsam mingling with the more pleasant smell of bacon and porky beans cooking at the fire. The red sun had his orb about level with the top of the divide.

As Dupuy later wrote: "We lay by the fire, relaxed our aching limbs, and let our eyes roam over the marsh, glittering with icicles and hoar frost crystals, that we had just crossed. The tea was steaming ready in the pail when, on a sudden, we were startled by the sound of falling stone tumbling down into the bottom of the ravine, followed by larger boulders. Then came a harsh and appalling roar. We sprang to our feet and I don't mind saying my teeth chattered and it was not with cold, either! Right across the ravine, on the side opposite to that where we were camped, the boulders were rolling heavily into the bottom, as a gigantic black and hairy animal slowly and heavily ascended the grade. From the corner of its mouth a bloodstained frothy slime dripped. Its horrid jaws were munching, munching, munching. The priest, the sourdough, and Buttler unconsciously clasped each other by the arms and tried to shout, but could not utter a sound. And well for us was it that they were stricken dumb! Our Indians crouched on the ground, their faces ashy and their bodies trembling like aspen leaves. They pressed their faces on the ground to shut out the sight. Buttler suddenly got up and tore down the hill.

UFOs Attack Earth ... The Out of Control Universe of Harold T. Wilkins

"Luckily, the monster had not sighted us! He stopped barely 100 paces from us. Then, propping his huge belly on a big flat rock, he stood motionless, gazing into the glaring eye of the red and setting sun! It was a sight that may have been not unfamiliar to our giant forefathers in a remote age. The monster stood still for ten minutes, as did we. He actually swiveled round his huge neck and still did not see us. I calculated he was around 50 feet long. He had a sort of rhinoceros horn on top of his jaws and his carcass was covered with black stiff bristles like those of a wild boar. The hair was plastered with mud and frozen muck. I'd put his weight at all of 50 tons.

"As we watched, a sound like the crunching of bones came from his dripping jaws. Then he reared on his hind legs, emitted a horribly hollow roar, gave a terrific leap, and vanished up the ravine. We made no attempt to follow him."

Dupuy and the party went to Dawson City and asked the governor to send out 50 armed men and mules, though it seems to me that a battery of howitzers would not have been amiss. The **Dawson City Daily Nugget** got hold of the story and likened Dupuy and party to Baron von Munchausen, Ananias, Barnum and Louis de Rougemont all rolled into one. Perhaps the governor of the Northwest Territories suspicioned a hoax, for he never gave the aid asked by Dupuy.

Yet the monster was seen again. About five years later, when Dupuy was back in France, he had a letter from Pere Lavagneux, who wrote:

"Ten of my Indians and myself have again seen that horrible beast of Partridge Creek. It was on Christmas Eve, and the monster was passing like a whirlwind over the frozen surface of the river, breaking off with his hind feet enormous blocks of ice from the frozen surface. His fur was covered with hoar frost and his little eyes—that was why he probably did not see us when we met him, some five years back when you were here, my son—glittered like fire in the dusk. He had in his jaws something which looked to me like a caribou. He moved at the rate of more than 30 miles an hour. The temperature stood at 45 degrees below zero. At the corner of the cut-off, the monster vanished.

"It is evidently the same monster we saw before. Together with the chief Stinehane and his two sons, I followed up the trail of the horrid beast. They were exactly like the tracks you and I and the rest saw when you were here. Then, they were embedded in the muck of the moose lick. Eight times on the snow we measured the prints. They were the same and so was the enormous body. Not the

20th of an inch difference! We trailed them to Stewart, fully three miles, when the snow fell and obliterated the tracks."

SPECULATION ON THE MYTH OR REALITY OF MODERN MONSTERS

Of course, readers may, like the **Dawson City Daily Nugget**, deem such a story all hooey, if not a hoax. Or they may ask us, "Where are the fathers, mothers, sisters, brothers, sons and daughters of these monsters? They cannot live *in vacuo*, nor were they unbegotten, uncreated, nor can they live eternally."

To which one may reply, with a shrug of the shoulder, "*Quien sabe?*"

Scientists and zoologists and paleontologists ridicule these stories, just as they derided Sir Harry Johnston's account of the central African okapi, until presently a specimen was found. Others may dismiss the stories as legends, or subjects for the psychologist rather than the biologist. How did such monsters escape the fate that befell their ancestors millions of years ago, when the oncoming of glaciation and the secular rise in the elevation of great landmasses spelled their doom? In the disappearance of lush vegetation and hot, steamy swamps and plains where the sun shone ever hot and bright from a cobalt sky, and rain fell, as it seems to do in Venus nearer the sun, only in warm showers in the night—how did they survive?

I have already suggested an answer to this question, above, but I may riposte, as a Scotchman would do, with a question in turn.

I may ask: are the monkey puzzle tree (Araucaria), of the temperate zone, and the Welwitchia (tumboa) of the South African deserts, the only survivors of the steaming life of hot swamps and torrid plains of the Mesozoic ages? Did the dinosaur, or the Pleistocene mammoths and mastodons leave no descendants behind them to inhabit lonely enclaves of lost worlds where climate and zoogeographical and geological conditions favored their survival?

UFOs Attack Earth ... The Out of Control Universe of Harold T. Wilkins

King Kong Lives!

This next section is one of the most thrilling so far! Harold T. Wilkins relates a series of true life, real time stories of encounters with living King Kong-type monsters in the jungles of Central and South America. There is the tale of how an unfortunate hunting guide is ripped to pieces by a large and hairy monster, and another story of an apelike beast who stripped the clothes off of several Mayan women in broad daylight, leaving them stark naked. Still another King Kong-like monstrosity terrorized a village for several nights, resulting in a mass exodus by the terrified natives. All of which combine to give us a fascinating glimpse into a truly out of control universe!

⚜ ⚜ ⚜

HAIRY KING KONG OF YUCATAN

Far south, in Yucatan, in the jungles and forests of the Mayas, among the limestone ranges with their great caverns, another beastly monster is stated to exist. His habitat is near the headwaters of the Rio Mopan, northwest of Arenal. No Indian will venture into the dense jungles and forests where this monster has his home. The late Dr. Thomas Gann, an archeologist and traveler who took part in more than one expedition organized by the British Museum, sought to encounter this beast. This thrilling story has been told by Frank Blaucaneaux, a naturalist who wrote "Biologica Americana Centrale." I give the story as I had it in Tegucigalpa, in Honduras.

Many years ago, Blaucaneaux and a Negro went up to the headwaters of the Rio Mopan to explore a region of thick and unknown forests where strange beasts and ancient ruins are believed to exist.

The weather was hot and sultry, and about noon Blaucaneaux and the black man pulled up in the middle of a grassy hollow, which appeared to be a windbreak cut by hurricanes in the forest. Towering up in the center of the glade was a lofty cohune palm, of Honduranian species. This tree's large nuts provide oil, and the tall smooth trunk a wood from which fancy articles are made. The hot rays of the sun shimmered on the leaves of the tall cottonwood in whose shade they lay. The heat was so great it made the men gasp.

They were about to fall into a siesta when their eyes were attracted to the cohune palm. Twenty feet or so above the ground, its leaves and branches were shaking as if some large animal were trying to make the tree shed its nuts. Blaucaneaux, glancing at the Negro, saw that his face had become ashy and that he was all a quiver with fright. His eyes were fairly bulging with fear.

"Say, Miguel, go and see what in hell is shakin' that tree," bade Blaucaneaux.

The Negro looked at the boss in an imploring manner, his eyes begging to be let off the job, although normally he was far from timorous.

"Debil debil, foh shuah, mastah," said the Negro, his teeth chattering.

Blaucaneaux laughed and ordered the Negro to get up and go to the foot of the palm. So, taking his rifle in his hand, the black man crept reluctantly toward the shaking tree. He had to force a way through grass as tall and spiky as any found in an African forest jungle.

Suddenly, an agonizing shriek rent the air, followed by dreadful groans. It was the voice of the black man, and he seemed to be in mortal pain. Blaucaneaux jumped up and shouldered his way through the tall grass, noting as he went that some large animal had made a previous track through it.

Under the cohune palm, poor Miguel, the black man, lay on his back, his shirt ripped to shreds, great red lanes running down his naked abdomen, and from his face to his breast, he was one mass of gory pulp. Blaucaneaux saw at a glance that the poor devil was dying. He had been disemboweled, and his entrails were protruding. He pried open the Negro's teeth and poured a little canna between his lips, and the dying man managed to whisper: "Black debil for shuah rip me up. Den run for bush."

Blaucaneaux buried the black man under the tree, regretting that he had been so insistent on sending him out on such an errand. Then he got up and trailed the monster through the bush. He was easy to follow. Branches, leaves and twigs, torn by the monster from trees he passed, strewed the path like leaves in the vale of Vallambrosa. The tracks passed out of the forest, over a savanna, and entered another zone of thick brush and forest, which ranged to the foot of

UFOs Attack Earth . . . The Out of Control Universe of Harold T. Wilkins

- 63 -

limestone crags more than five miles away. Here, the monster entered the bed of a donga, or dried bed of a brook, cluttered with big boulders, some of which he had evidently turned over, as if searching for tasty food.

Realizing the risk he was running, Blaucaneaux kept his eyes alert. It was obvious that even an express rifle bullet might not stop so formidable a beast if he discovered a hunter was on his trail.

It was near on dusk when Blaucaneaux stood before the entrance of a big cave in the limestone *cerro*. Owing to the peculiar geological formation of these limestone ranges in Yucatan, Guatemala and Honduras, such caves ramify and often stretch for miles in a labyrinth of man-high passages and regular catacombs. A man may easily lose himself in them, and to encounter a monster—such as the one who had disemboweled the Negro—in a confined space, would be suicide. The light was dim, and Blaucaneaux entered the cavern after lighting with a match a bit of an old Mexican newspaper he had in his pocket.

He whistled in surprise. The cavern floor was wet and slimy with the water percolating from the roof. In the soft white mud he saw prints, which, he said: "Were like the thumb and two fingers of a large human hand. Each finger was armored with terrible claws."

Wisely, Blaucaneaux decided to call it a day and to quit the cave while the going was good. He had no fancy to come to close quarters with those terrible claws, and be in the grip of a monster who must be a sort of King Kong of the Maya land. On the way back, he became bogged in the forest and had to use a compass to find his way out.

Later, he tried to induce Indians to accompany him on the trail for the cohune palm, and the cave of the hairy monster; but the wise Indians "were not having any." Blaucaneaux's plan, not a promising one, was to smoke the monster out and block up the cave entrance. What, however, the monster would have been doing all the while this crazy plan was being carried out, Blaucaneaux did not stop to think. It is safe to say hairy King Kong of the Maya forest and caves would neither have kissed nor hugged them, and any glad hand he tendered would surely have had armored claws! In a word, he would have made some of them into what the old English housewife in a western cathedral city where the present writer spent his boyhood, called "prime chitterlings."

HAIRY KING KONG DISROBES AND SHAKES UP MAYAN WOMEN

Dr. Gann, who visited Arenal at a later date, went up the Rio Mopan, and heard that native women in the bush had been most ungallantly seized from behind by some formidable hairy animal, black as the devil, who came suddenly on them in the daytime. The monster tore off all their clothes till the women were stark naked. Then he clutched them in his hairy arms and shook them good and hard till their teeth rattled. Having completed that part of his beauty treatment, he carried them well into the thick and thorny bush and dropped them in disgust. The women described the monster as of immense size, covered with stiff black hair, and said he obviously had a strong objection to clothes.

An Indian told Gann that his tribe had come on a large tree in the forest with rough bark. About six feet from the ground, the bark was found to be covered with long, black stiff hairs coated with a white powder like lime. Gann was never able to trail down the cave of the hairy monster of the Mopan. Therefore, he waits for some late 20th century Barnum to bring him back alive. That is, if he can find him and isn't killed in the effort! While trying to locate this "hairy devil," Gann also lit on strange tracks in the Mayan jungle which singularly resembled those of the giant iguanodon, hitherto believed to be extinct.

TEDDY ROOSEVELT MAKES VOYAGE DOWN "RIVER OF DOUBT"

Earlier in this story, the reader will recall that I spoke of a "Lost World" in part of the 1.5 million square miles of the unexplored Roosevelt-Goyaz plateau of central Brazil. As far back as 1913, Theodore Roosevelt and his son, accompanied by General Candino Rondon, the Brazilian Indian who has given his name to the vast area of Brazil called Rondonia, explored the western edge of this unknown region, when they went down the "River of Doubt"—later called the Rio Roosevelt. This river falls into the Rio Madeira, a tributary of the mighty Rio Maranon, or Amazon.

The group traveled 900 miles through difficult country, made portages over many catadupas, or rapids, and lost most of their supplies. Fever struck most of the party down, and they had many of their canoes to sink beneath them. Even so, the Roosevelt party touched merely the edge of this blank space on the map of Brazil.

EXPLORERS DISAPPEAR DURING SEARCH FOR DEAD CITY

The Indians of the forests of the Matto Grosso say that a great cataclysm drove forth into this wilderness, thousands of years ago, a great white race who ruled their ancestors from great walled cities. The region became one of vast swamps and deep jungles where giant saurians, extinct elsewhere in the world in the long ago, wallowed or walked the beaches of great reedy lagoons. Also, monstrous animals moved into the ruins as they became covered with dense bush and jungle.

In 1925, the British Colonel Philip Henry Fawcett, his son, and a young Los Angeles chap, named Raleigh Rimell, vanished into this unknown from the jumping-off place of Cuyaba. They planned to locate one of the dead cities; but I have reason to suppose that two of the party became the victims of head-hunters of the Kaingang tribes, owing, so I heard in Rio de Janeiro, to a violation by a young fellow of a tabu.

Fourteen years earlier, Colonel Fawcett, who was an experienced explorer, scientist and geographer, and far from any fly-by-night adventurer, explored the Caupolican—a region little known today—in eastern Bolivia. He was near the Rio Heath, when, one day, he came on a large reedy and swampy lagoon in the forest, and in the slime of the beach was startled to observe "tracks huge and unrecognizable," as of some monster like a dinosaur. The Indians also assert that other fearsome animals inhabit the unknown tableland lying farther east in central Brazil.

UFOs Attack Earth . . . The Out of Control Universe of Harold T. Wilkins

APE MAN'S REIGN OF TERROR ON RIO ARAGUAYAN BORDER

Point was given to these rumors, in March 1937, when a queer story was cabled from Rio de Janeiro. It told of a regular King Kong, a match for the famous monster of the well-known film suggested by the late British novelist, Edgar Wallace. It was said that this immense ape-like creature had swooped down from the tableland and started a reign of terror in the area bordering on the Rio Araguaya. He was heard in the night, on the outskirts of lonely aldeias, roaring like a thousand lions. Terrified villagers barred themselves up.

After a night of panic, the villagers ventured out of their houses at dawn to find dozens of hardy Spanish cattle and yellow steers lying dead on the pampas—their tongues torn out. In the ground near the carcasses of the cattle, they saw manlike imprints of feet about one-and-a-half feet long. Perhaps the monster making such prints would be more than 12 feet tall. What was odd was that the fierce cattle had apparently made no struggle with the monster, which had leapt out on them from the darkness of the night. Yet it must be remembered that these cattle will charge a jaguar or any man who happens to be caught out on the pampas unmounted.

Night after night the monster returned, and the roarings and howlings he uttered were diabolical. A regular exodus began. No one would stay in the villages. Three weeks passed, and then came a report—which I have never been able to confirm—that King Kong had been captured. It was said that a horse he had killed bore on his back the imprint of a monstrous humanlike hand.

SEX RELATIONS BETWEEN GIANT APES AND INDIAN WOMEN; THEIR HYBRID PROGENY

In the state of Panama, well out of the Canal Zone, is an ancient stone idol carved by a race unknown, about whom not even the dimmest tradition exists. Close to the image stands the figure of an unknown monster on a pillar whereon hieroglyphs are also carved. It may remind us that in various little known regions of Ecuador, Colombia and Costa Rica there, today, exist giant anthropoid apes, unknown to any zoo park or natural history museum. Such apes are found in the Nicoya peninsula of Costa Rica, but they are not to be identified with the malos hombres, or "gorillas" who have come to this region from places in Nicaragua elsewhere, too hot to hold them. The peninsula runs from north to south, along the Pacific. In the Tarro River area of this region is found a giant, black and hairy ape, of unknown American anthropoid species.

In the old days of the Spanish conquistadors in South America, stories were rife of sexual intercourse between large apes and Indian women. The stories do not seem to seem to have been altogether fantastic. For the old cronista and soldier, Pedro Cieza de Leon says—without supporting evidence—he personally met some of these women and saw their hybrid progeny, whose "language" consisted of horrid moans and howls, in the deep woods.

Anthropoids, Giants and Mammoths

In this chapter taken from Harold T. Wilkins' "monsters booklet," Wilkins continues to press the point that various so-called "prehistoric" monsters, long thought to predate mankind by millions of years, were instead contemporaneous with ancient man, who shared the planet with these bizarre beasts in an uneasy truce that often spilled over into warfare. The hardy ancients left behind many artifacts attesting to their daily struggle with mammoths and mastodons and the ever-present large apes, if only we are open to their ghostly testimony.

THADDEUS O'SHEA'S NON-AMOROUS CONTACT WITH ANTHROPOID

In 1633, an expedition of Spanish soldiers in the Bahia de los Pinos, in southwestern Darien, province of old Panama, went ashore, and in the woods captured a large giant black ape, of a sort which, in parts of ancient Mexico exist, or used to exist, in images of stone. A fearsome giant ape of this type exists, today, in the unknown and unexplored region up the Rio Sambu, in southwestern Panama. I heard of an American old-timer and prospector who had an adventure, by no means amorous, with one of these giant anthropoids. He told the yarn in a hospital in Panama City, in 1920.

He, Thaddeus O'Shea, had been hunting gold and rare birds and butterflies in regions where the Indians shoot intruders at sight and ask questions afterwards. O'Shea reached a ruined and ancient city, where, in a lagoon, he saw a giant lizard which skated, so he said, upright over waters covered with lilies and alive with brilliantly plumaged wild ducks. But there came a time when he decided it was fitting to make for the someplace on the coast visited by an occasional banana boat from Balboa. Long was it since he had tasted rye, Bourbon or Scotch whiskey. He had a nugget or two in his old poke and a tin of gold dust, and he might call it a day and quit a country where he had found the Indians most unfriendly to men not of their color.

Some weeks later, he reached the headwaters of the Rio Sambu, where he lit on an old dugout canoe. Whittling paddles from branches, he canoed the crazy contraption downstream. Unluckily, the canoe hit a snag in the river and overset with most of his equipment. All he saved were a nugget in his pouch, a pinch of gold dust in an old needle case, and a pistol with a round or two of ammunition.

One hot evening, he reached the top of a divide and halted to make a hut of leaves and boughs. There he decided to camp for the night.

Howler monkeys screamed and roared in the surrounding woods, and their tune was not that which would have met with the approval of the Ancient Mariner, in the leafy month of June. To make things more lively, the cicadas whistling like a small steamboat siren kept him awake, though really he had been long enough in the country to have got used to such nocturnal orchestras. Yet sleep he could not. Still, he was not troubled with the sort of conscience that makes for insomnia. So his senses were alert, when, about midnight, an odd noise caused him to sit up on his couch of leaves. Outside the hut some large animal was lumbering around. He judged its size by the way it was trampling down the bushes. But he had been long enough in the tropics to know the folly of interfering with large animals before they interfered with you. He turned round and fell asleep.

Came dawn and Thaddeus came out of his hut to get water from the river. He had climbed to the top of a bush-crowned ridge overlooking the bank, when he halted in his tracks. On top of the ridge, there stood glaring at him a monstrous black man, all of eight feet high. He stood erect and was covered with long black hair and gibbered at him in rage. Suddenly, the monster raised his arms and was clearly contemplating a charge downhill on top of Thaddeus. Quick as lightning, our hero pulled out his pistol, which fortunately was loaded, and shot the monster through the head. He spun round like a teetotum and fell dead. As soon as Thaddeus recovered from the shock and steadied his shaking limbs, he ran a cord around the monster, which had the chest of a Congo gorilla. But its big toes were human, not like those of the ordinary ape.

UFOs Attack Earth . . . The Out of Control Universe of Harold T. Wilkins

It may be noted that figures of large apes appear in old Mayan statues.

GIANT MEN, MAMMOTHS, MASTADONS IN AMERO-INDIAN MYTHS

The mammoth and the mastodon figure largely in Amero-Indian myths and are found in far more ancient glyphs, pictographs, and are carved on idols of far earlier date, in various regions of the U.S.A.

The Oneida Indians had a tradition about a mammoth—as it seems from the story—who invaded the settlements of their ancestors, and, off the shores of Lake Ontario, showed such rage that he pulled down houses and cabins, then forced people to flee from his hell-raising to the shelter of stockaded forts. Warriors were bowled over like nine-pins, caught up to a huge trunk, whirled around and dashed to the ground or stamped into the earth.

This raging juggernaut stayed around until a chief collected men, fought a severe battle, and forced the monster to retire.

On the walls of the Supai Canyon, in Arizona, is a petroglyph, not so ancient as that of the dinosaur to which I have referred above. It depicts a mammoth with a long trunk in the act of attacking a man who, by the relative sizes, must have been a giant. And, reader, giants have existed in both North and South and Central America, where, in recent years, remains, such as bone and patterned pottery, have been found, as in the Sierra Madre in an ancient cemetery in the Yaqui country of Sonora, and far south, along the railroad at Manta, Ecuador. All of which shows that the men and women to whom they belonged were from eight to nine feet high.

The Lenape stone, found on a farm in Pennsylvania, in 1872, shows a fight between savages and a hairy mammoth on the edge of the forest. The monster has his tail erect, in a great rage. He is approaching the forest, and between the trees can be glimpsed wigwams and tents. Again, Indian tribes of Canada's northwestern territory say their ancestors, thousands of years ago, had to take refuge in the middle of lakes, where they built huts on piles because the countryside around was ravaged with vast, hairy animals with trunks.

Writers in the early 19th century were sometimes apt to talk as if the mammoth and mastodon were carnivorous animals, whereas they were herbivorous. Nor ought this too surprise us when we recall that vegetarians of the modern human species are often apt to be more provocative and aggressive than meat-eaters. As experience shows, the fiercest and most gory fights have often arisen at meetings addressed by vegetarians styling themselves pacifists.

The wooly mammoth, as distinct from the mastodon, possessed a long, curving tusk. There is good evidence, both in North and South America, that both the mammoth and the mastodon were contemporary with ancient man. In old Europe, in fact, a well-known artifact in the shape of a chunk of ivory skillfully carved by a Paleolithic artist has a lively representation of a mammoth's head and tusk. The artist saw him in the region of what are now the Pyrenees Mountains, on the border of France and Spain. But, in North America, these monsters existed at a far later date. In Oregon, the mastodon's bones were found near Silver Lake mixed with flint arrows and spearheads. The Ohio Indians said the mastodon went to sleep leaning against the trunk of a tree. He might be ready for whatever enemy came his formidable way. The early Indians in the Mississippi Valley were contemporary with both monsters, and Jefferson speaks of a Mr. Stanley captured by Indians at the mouth of the Tennessee River and carried westwards beyond the Missouri, where the Indians told him the monster still lived in the north. They gave him a description of an animal which appeared to be a large elephant.

DO MASTODONS STILL LIVE—
AND SHED THEIR TEETH IN THE ANDES?

The Jesuit missionary, Pere Charlevoix, in Canada, about 1744, heard an Indian tradition about a monster elephant of such immense size that other species seemed like ants beside him. Said the Indians: "He has legs so high that eight feet of snow do not embarrass him, and his skin is proof against all sorts of weapons. He has also a sort of arm which comes out from his shoulder, and which he uses as we do ours."

Here, they may have crystallized an ancient memory of the wooly mammoth. In remote places, the mastodon seems to have lasted into quite modern times. Indeed, even today, he is rumored to exist high up in little-known recesses of the Andes in Colombia.

In 1820, a British royal navy captain, Charles Stuart Cochrane, told how, when he was in the valley of Ubate, in Columbia, South America, he was told that, close to a snow-covered sierra, towering over the valley, the natives had seen, through a good glass, "numbers of carnivorous elephants feeding on the plains which skirt these frozen regions, their enormous teeth having been occasionally seen, but no one has yet succeeded in killing one of these animals, or, indeed, in getting near them."

Cochrane does not say that he himself saw them, but John Rankine, who wrote, in 1827, "Historical Researches Concerning the Conquest of Peru," said that mastodons were still living in the Andes, and "shed their teeth." Thomas Jefferson wrote: "The traditionary testimony of the Indians is that the mammoth still exists in the northern and western parts of America. He may well exist in those unexplored parts now, as formerly he did, where now we find his bones."

Trappers in the far north and in northern British Columbia believe that mammoths and mastodons are alive at this day in remote regions in Alaska and the Yukon Territory, but offer no evidence.

TRADER (ALOYSIUS) HORN SOUNDS OFF

That old trader, Aloysius Horn, whose real life was probably far more hectic and less respectable than the story he put forth at second-hand to the world, was speaking, in the 1930s, of Darkest Africa, when he said to the South American authoress who wrote up his life: "Ave, Africa's a strange place, ma'am. I believe there's beasts still living in the dark places and lakes that no white man's ever seen."

MASTODON BONES AT BOTTOM OF MINE SHAFT IN ZULULAND

Indeed, Africa has many tales of these monsters of lost worlds and vast steamy swamps in its equatorial zones. In November, 1929, a party of explorers, wandering in the Tugela Valley of Zululand, strayed up a lonely and almost inaccessible gorge, where they lit on the mouth of an ancient and long disused mineshaft. (Author's note by Harold T. Wilkins: Farther north are the mysterious ruins of Zimbabwe, built by extremely ancient gold miners of some white, civilized race of whom no satisfactory account has ever been given. The race, as to its origins, is one of Africa's darkest mysteries.)

At the bottom of the shaft, the explorers found crude picks and crucibles of ancient gold miners, who were certainly *not* from among the local native population. Among the debris at the bottom of the ancient shaft were human bones, and alongside lay the vast jaws and ribs of a huge prehistoric mastodon, which crashed to his doom ages ago, and clearly long after the ancient miners had abandoned the workings.

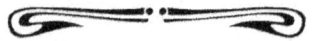

UFOs Attack Earth... The Out of Control Universe of Harold T. Wilkins

Live Monsters And Other Creatures Of Africa

Do monsters still live in the unexplored regions of Africa? According to these stories from Harold T. Wilkins' rare and hard to find booklet, living monsters continue to be a tantalizing possibility. Everything from a bottomless black pit said to house just such a monster to a creature called a Nandi bear that drops from the trees onto the shoulders of hapless natives is included here. What the natives shirk from in terror, some foolish white men blindly pursue!

GATTI PROBES PIT IN LIVINGSTONE ROCKS OF NORTHERN RHODESIA

Commander Attilio Gatti, in July, 1930, was hunting for signs of prehistoric man in and around the famous Livingstone Rocks in Northern Rhodesia. Gatti and a pal wandered off the track into the Mumba Cavern, which is located in the middle of a great swamp tenanted by ferocious reptiles and carnivorous land beasts, not to speak of vile insects with pathogenic probes. He presently started up a splendid golden-maned lion, a grinning lioness and four fine cubs, which, luckily for him—for he had only a small bore gun—vanished into the bush with a whisk of their angry tales. Here, a low-browed black praiser of past days among the tribal chiefs told Gatti of another deep and mysterious hole in the hills near by.

"This, boss, be called Kawena," said the chief, with a queer smile. "One time, bad man be made to jump in there."

"Oh, and how?" queried Gatti.

The black man, with a series of pantomimic gestures that would have made his fortune in a wild Africa show, indicated how, for years past, scallywags in the kraals (stockaded villages of equatorial Africa) had been rounded up and forced to jump into a great chasm. The Negro swore, with rolling eyes, that a strange monster—some dragon Grendel—lived at the bottom of the immensely deep pit.

Gatti was interested. He took a long rope, and while the guides stayed well away from the pit, he got a friend to lower him into this abyss. As he went, he startled crowds of mephitic bats which were clinging to the sides of the precipice. At last, more than 80 feet down, the rope petered out and left Gatti hanging in the air, trying vainly with his eyes to pierce the darkness to where he presumed the bottom lay. He saw none—only black darkness. He said he was sure that many grim relics and macabre remains must be strewing the bottom of that unplumbed hole. Perhaps on the floor of the chasm lay skulls of great ethnic and geological interest, or remains of civilized and unknown races that have vanished in the night of time. Some day he hoped to return and find out if some fearsome monster really did have his lair in that abyss.

ELEPHANT GRAVEYARDS, LIVE MONSTERS OF KALAHARI DESERT

Queer tales are told of the great wastes of the Kalahari Desert of South Africa, habitat of platinum, gold, and diamonds and the queer pygmies called the Bushmen. Somewhere in its fastnesses are said to be great elephant cemeteries, where solitary elephants go to die when they feel their days are ended and where tons of ivory are alleged to abound. Within the region of these swamps is a lake called Ngami, said to be a lost world of hot steaming marsh where still lives more than one brontosaurus of the Mesozoic ages. These monsters are said to have trekked to the swamps, ages ago, from what was the location of the modern Orange River.

UFOs Attack Earth . . . The Out of Control Universe of Harold T. Wilkins

MESOZOIC MONSTERS PHOTOGRAPHED IN DILOLO SWAMPS OF CONGO

In 1932, wild takes reached Cape Town, South Africa, that one of these mysterious monsters had been seen in the vast Dilolo swamps of the Congo. He had been sought by a young game-hunter, Frederick Grobler, who had gone there for the purpose. Grobler failed in his search, but met Negroes who were convinced of its existence, and said it was called the "chepekwe." They also called it the "sea lion." Grobler's story had been dismissed as a fantasy, when there one day appeared in a Johannesburg newspaper a photograph of which showed a huge reptile, or giant lizard, feeding off the carcass of a dead hippopotamus which lay rotting in a swamp. The cameraman was said to be a German scientist who first discovered that the monster existed in the Dilolo swamps. Of course, photographs are often faked.

It was now stated that Grobler had been acting as guide to the German Schomburghk expedition, which spent a year filming wild animals in Central Africa, and had gone to the Dilolo swamps in order to film the "chepekwe." The leader of the expedition, Major Schomburghk, made a speech in Berlin, Germany, in which he said if anything could induce him to return to the Congo swamps, it would be the hope that he could film this carnivorous monster, who seemed to be a survivor of the age of the dinosaurs.

Some time later, photographs appeared in German newspapers, which stated that they had had them from a Swedish overseer of a rubber plantation in the Kassai district of Central Africa. The photographs depicted the "chepekwe." The sender, Mr. J.C. Johansen, wrote that, on February 16, 1932, he went on a shooting trip into the region of the Dilolo swamps. One day, he saw two elephants and behind them a strange beast of around 16 yards long, with a reptilian head and tail. Standing behind some tall elephant grass and high reeds, Johansen said he snapped his camera three times on the scene, but only one picture came out well. The monster, as he watched, gave great bounds and moved with amazing speed. He did not report whether the monster made any attack on the elephants and what their reaction was to its presence.

Johansen was badly scared and started on his way back out of the swamps. He was traversing a big marsh with reedy beds when he had a shock. Some yards away, its belly and sides plastered with oozy muck, he again saw the monster, this time banqueting off the carcass of a dead rhinoceros. From behind some thorny scrub, Johansen, scared as he was, did not forget business. He trained his camera on the munching monster—which seems to prefer rotting meat to fresh, in which, by the way, it shares the tastes of some of our own remote ancestors of the cave age, for whom the "higher" the meat, the greater the joy—and got some good pictures.

He stayed hidden until the monster disappeared, when he made rapid tracks for home, saying: "I've sure had a jolly good day today. Couldn't ha' been better!" Johansen, however, added that what he saw so greatly shocked him that he collapsed and was unconscious for nearly eight days.

Museum officials and zoologists in South Africa were skeptical. They said that while there was no reason that animals unknown to science should not still exist, it was yet unlikely that such a monster could exist in Africa—for six months—without scientists becoming aware of it. May be. But, it must be said that scientists said just this same thing about the okapi, and about the Komodo Dragon, before Sir Harry Johnston discovered an okapi, and the American explorer, Lawrence Griswold, brought one of the dragons home alive to the New York Zoo Park. A mere denial is not a rebuttal of the existence of the monster. It remains for some live American cinema-men to go out to the Dilolo swamps and take a film of the "chepekwe."

EAST AFRICA'S "WILDERNESS" OF ENDLESS WATERS AND STEAMY MARSH

In August, 1930, George Mossop, a big game hunter and trapper in Equatorial Africa, went into what is described as "a wilderness of endless waters and steamy marsh," in the hinterland of Beira, Portuguese East Africa. The region, which is shunned by Negroes, stretches far inland from the Indian Ocean and is populated by an immense multitude of frogs. A party of Britishers and black men led by Mossop spent a night on an old ant-heap in this great swamp. The ant-heap had been made many hundreds of years ago at a time when the locality was dry land.

About midnight, the party, dozing uneasily on the hillock, were roused by a strange noise coming a long way over the swamp. It was the muffled bellow or roar of some monstrous creature acting as a sort of obbligato to the lesser orchestra of the croaking and whistling frogs. It came only at intervals, rumbling above the chorus of the frogs. Suddenly, there came a startling hiss which cut through the frogs' concert like a knife. It seemed to be directed at the hillock on which the men stood. The black men at once left their side of the hillock and in terror crawled over to that where the white men stood. They wanted company. The sounds seemed to come from deep water. Mossop ordered the Negroes to collect fuel from dry trees and make a fire. As the flames shot up and crackled, loud hisses were heard. There were three of them of quite appalling character. Then came a noise of some Herculean body moving rapidly through the water. The night was too black for anything to be glimpsed. The marsh, even today, remains unexplored.

FIND MADE NEAR PYRAMID IN BURIED EGYPTIAN BOAT

Another reminder of strange and unknown monsters which ancient Africa once possessed, and may still possess today in unexplored regions round Lake Rudolph in what is northern Kenya, where it is joined by the frontiers of southern Abyssinia and the Sudan—was the discovery in May, 1935, by the Egyptian professor, Selim Hassan, of "day and night boats" used by the ancient Pharaohs in rites connected with the Egyptian underworld of the dead, or solar ceremonialism. Close to the pyramid of Chephren, Professor Hassan found a boat in which was the head of a gigantic animal with huge teeth. Its identity has not been established. The boat was found buried north of the temple of the ancient pyramid.

MYSTERY OF THE "NANDI BEAR"

The mystery of the "Nandi Bear," or "chemisette," still remains unsolved. This monster is said to walk on his hind legs and to attack women and children at sight and to jump down from trees onto the shoulders of native men. His home is said to be in the forest of Nandi, in upper Kenya. Natives, haunted by fears of spooks, will not venture into this forest where white hunters report they have come across strangely shaped footprints larger than those of a lion, but feline in character. The monster reminds us of Thomas Jefferson's "megalonyx," referred to earlier. It is his habit of dropping down from trees and clawing men to death that has made the natives shuns the places where he is supposed to live. He is said to be larger than a polar bear—but a bear with the head of a lion. The last expedition, of which I have any knowledge, to seek for this monster, started out from London, in December 1933, led by a young fellow named Richard Hamilton. He planned to make a jump-off into the wilds from Kitali on the Kenya railroad, which is a trek of 200 miles stretching towards the mysterious Lake Rudolph, and the "lost world" somewhere in its recesses. Seeking to unravel its mysteries, a number of white explorers mysteriously disappeared in the years 1934 and 1937. "Their canoes floating upside down, and their hats were picked up, owners believed dead," said a laconic cable from Mombassa to London. Indeed, youth has no need of world wars for an outlet for its valor and energies. There are, as I have shown, still spots on this earth where danger and mystery exist in plenty.

However, it may be said that zoologists are skeptical about the Nandi. They have been so ever since a game warden in Nairobi sent to a London journal a drawing of what he thought to be the Nandi's spoor. The spoor was five-and-a-half inches long and had six toes, which made Mr. R.I. Pocock, of the British Natural History Museum, suspect that the spoor was really that of two hyenas, superimposed. Skins said to be the Nandis' have also been identified, in London, as those of the rufous-tinted, spotted hyena of Somaliland. Yet, the question remains open; for it is a fact that even the redoubtable Masai native warriors of upper Kenya, who attack a full-grown, or man-eating lion, with spears alone, will not enter any forest where the Nandi bear is believed to lurk.

UFOs Attack Earth ... The Out of Control Universe of Harold T. Wilkins

Fearsome Creatures Great And Small

Africa and Australia are the locales of some more bizarre monsters sightings. Harold T. Wilkins has again captured some extremely strange moments of history and folklore, and the creatures herein described are the sort of thing that kept old-time explorers and prospectors awake at night, listening for the sound of the terrifying scuttling of their nightmares returning to haunt them.

BLACK "CHRISTIANS" OF LIBERIA SHOCK ARAB INFIDELS

Over on the west coast of Africa is Liberia, where, in a recent year, the Christian black men showed such gross inhumanity to the primitive "savages" of the bush in the interior, that even the reluctant admiration of scoundrelly Arab slave-raiders—who ravage Ethiopia and rape the handsome women of the Gallas—was aroused. It may be said, in passing, that in September, 1947, taking advantage of the absence of British naval patrols in the Red Sea, these Arabs were back at their old trade shipping black slaves to harems in the Hadramaut and Yemen of Arabia. They seemed to meet no hindrance from the black Christian. Ras Tafari, the "Lion of Judah," emperor of Abyssinia. Somebody must have had a rake-off on this traffic, connived at because these black men are "not Christians."

MARINE MONSTER OF THE JU-JU ROCK

But Liberia, say trappers, has other sorts of monsters than human blackamoors of "civilized sort." Far up a little-known river called the Cavally, on the frontiers of the French Ivory Coast, are creeks festooned from bank to bank with creepers that stifle trees whose branches join in such dense foliage that even the hot equatorial sun's rays cannot penetrate the dark arcades below. This river comes from the little-known Niam Mountains, still unexplored, even today. In the upper reaches of the Cavally, at the spot where it is called the Youbou, or Nion, is a strange rock called Ju-Ju. Natives, who paddle various sorts of nuts and copra down to coastal trading stations, say that all round the rock the water bubbles and boils like a maelstrom. They say—and there is an English trader who supports the story—that a great gray monster of dinosaur type shows his vast bulk under water, near the rock, and upturns any canoe nearby. He seems to be carnivorous, and is far too large to be any sort of crocodile. It may be said that here, that similar stories are told of the Rio Araguaya, in the Matto Grosso of Brazil, where a great reptile has been known to rise up from water near a cachoeira (rapids) and to have overturned a whole boatload of diamond diggers in quite recent years.

THE FEARSOME NZUDU'S HORN ERECTS

Still another strange African animal, who would fetch a fabulous price if any trapper could capture him, is the mysterious Nzudu. A certain Dr. Andrew Smith, cited about 1860 a Madagascar missionary, who, he says: "Was told by a native that, in a region north of Mozambique, in Portuguese East Africa, was a strange quadruped, called the Nzoodoo, which was not rare in Makooa. He was as big as a horse, extremely swift, strong, and with a horn about two feet three inches long in his forehead. The horn lay depressed when the strange beast slept, curled up like an elephant's proboscis. If he were enraged, the horn was erected stiff and hard. The Nzoodoo was extremely fierce and attacked men at sight. When natives were attacked by him, they climbed a thick tall tree out of sight. But if the monster sighted anyone in the tree, he at once began a frontal attack of the tree with his horn, bored a hole in the root, brought the tree crashing to the ground, and gored or mangled the black to death."

Baron von Muller wrote, some years earlier—in 1849—to a London journal, and said he had talked with a Negro in Kordofan, in central Sudan, who offered him the pelt of an animal called the anasa, who seems to be a species of Nzudu. Said the baron: "This strange animal is the size of a smaller ass, and has a tail like that of a boar. He has a long horn in the forehead, which hangs loose in a state of quiescence, but is erect at once if he sees a man. The horn is a formidable weapon, but I do not know its exact length. I have often seen it in wild grounds, where the Negroes kill it and make shields from its skin."

One may observe that Dr. Andrew Smith's testimony about the Nzudu would not, for obvious reasons, be accepted in a court of law; but here is Sir John Barrow, author of "Travels In Africa," who says he saw inside a cavern a Kaffir's sketch of an animal like the Nzudu. The reader will also recall the story of David Ingram of an animal he saw in North America—mentioned above—which strangely recalls the African Nzudu. But it may be said that the little-known learned author of the late 15th or early 16th century, Ludovicus Varlomannus, who wrote in Latin, says he saw two strange animals, resembling the Nzudu, which had been sent from Ethiopia to the Sultan of Turkey and "kept in a repository in Mahomet's tomb in Mecca"; and Petrus Martyrus de Anghiera, better known as Peter Martyr, wrote, about 1520, that: "He lives in wild desolate places in Africa, has a long snout like an elephant, color of an ox, hoof of a horse, ears not so open as those of an elephant, yet hanging down much under those of any other beast."

After this, I can but advise the skeptic to take the long trail from New York to Kordofan and Lake Rudolph, or Ethiopia, and fetch one back alive. Fame and fortune awaits such man or woman, not to speak of box office riots calculated to convince any tough guy in Hollywood.

IN THE HINTERLAND OF MADAGASCAR —A MONSTER BIRD

In that strange lumber-room of evolution and missing links, the still little explored hinterland of Madagascar, there may sometime be discovered dead, if not alive, the tremendous wingless bird, called the Aepyornis. This may be the bird called the Roc, in the Arabian Nights' story of Sinbad the Sailor, and it is likely that the famous Venetian traveler, Marco Polo, saw this tremendous bird in an island off Madagascar. He called it the Roc. This bird stood seven feet high, and distantly resembled the emu, or the mandu of old South Africa. In the Malagassy glens, the Aepyornis could easily carry on its back a large buck or full-grown antelope. Its very eggs were eight times the size of those of a modern ostrich, and when blown could hold two gallons of liquid.

The Aepyornis had some prodigious cousins, in the South Pacific and in West Australia, which must have been much alive in the middle of the 17th century, and in 1768-1771, when the well-known round-the-world navigator, the British Captain James Cook, first sailed the South Seas. It was a Dutch burgomaster of Amsterdam, however, Mr. Witsen, who wrote to the Royal Society of London about a strange gigantic bird's nest found by the Hollanders when they landed on the coast of Nova Hollandia, or Western Australia, in 1696. Says he: "A Dutch East India sloop sent into the South Land, called Hollandia Nova, in 1696, to get intelligence of a ship lost with Sir James Cooper and 300 men thought to be stranded there, but since understood to be taken by pirates, near Madagascar, and Sir James by them killed, found birds' nests of a prodigious greatness that six men could not, stretching out their arms, encompass one of the nests. But the fowls were not to be found."

About 75 years later, an Englishman, A. Kippis, member of the British Royal Society, described how a remarkable discovery was made of Captain Cook's first voyage to the Southern Pacific. He writes: "Mr. Banks and Lieutenant Cook landed in a low sandy island in the Endeavor River and found the nest of some bird, of what species they could not determine; but it must have been certainly one of the largest kinds that ever existed. This was apparent from the enormous size of the nest, which was built with sticks on the ground, and which was no less than 26 feet in circumference, and two feet eight inches high. They called the spot Eagle Island."

A gigantic bird of this sort was described by Henderson, an English traveler, who went into New Siberia, in the 18th century. He says he met with the claws of a bird which were three feet long, which was equivalent to the size of the toes of a mammoth measured by Dr. Adam Clark in North America, in 1830. The Yakuts told Henderson that often when out hunting they found the skeleton and even the feathers of this giant bird, the quills of which were large enough to "admit a man's arm into the caliber."

THE DINORNIS OF NEW ZEALAND IS A NIGHT BIRD

The Dinornis or Moa, was another Australian gigantic bird which existed down to modern times. It stood 16 feet high. In 1842, a New Zealand parson, the Rev. Peter Williams, wrote: "I was told that the Dinornis still lived at a hill called Wakapunak, where it was guarded by a lizard, or large reptile. But no one alive seems to have seen it. I have offered a reward for its capture, or that of the reptile. I sent to England the bones of a dead Moa, which reached 16 feet."

English and American whalers were said to have seen this giant bird near Cloudy Bay, Cook's Straits, New Zealand. It could be seen only at night, when two Englishmen and a native Maori saw it some way off. It stood from 14 to 16 feet high. One sailor proposed to approach an shoot it, but the others, who were scared at its size, would not agree. The bird presently stood took alarm and strode off up the side of a mountain. Prior to 1880, Dr. Hector, a government geologist, in New Zealand, found their tracks in the middle of an island. The print of the claws measured 15 inches long, while the length of the stride was nearly six feet. Old time diggers say they have seen this gigantic bird at the dusk of evening, or by the light of their campfires. They are night birds, solitary in their habits and hard to approach. The stuffed remains of one of these giant Moas is, or used to be seen, in a museum at Oxford, England, and a live specimen was once brought to England for show.

The British Museum used to have a stuffed specimen of the dodo, but one summer a cleaner thought the old moth-eaten skin was not worth keeping and threw it into a rubbish heap. Now, no money can purchase a specimen of this giant bird, and the museum has only an imperfect skeleton.

"KADITCHA"—THE LAND OF EVIL THINGS

Australia has long had its stories of monster animals and saurians which scare the life out of prospectors in its lone fastnesses. Even scientists did not disdain to investigate such a story which reached Melbourne in October, 1931, when Mr. Fred Blakeley, leader of the Centralian Gold Exploration Expedition, said he had measured the tracks of an amazing and ferocious reptile called the "prenty." The monster inhabits the tract of broken country which lies in the heart of Central Australia, some 350 miles long by 250 miles wide. The aboriginal black fellows shun the region, which they call "Kaditcha," the land of evil things. Blakeley was hunting for opals in the Stuart Range, when he met with "Big Jim," an old fossicker, or prospector, who stands nearly seven feet in his socks and weighs 18 stone. "Big Jim" is sure a tough guy, but even he had had a rare fright. Here is this story of his hectic adventure:

"I was one day walkin' along scannin' the ground for signs of opals, when I spun round at the hearin' of a queer sound. I sure shook in my boots! There was an enormous reptile reared up on a ridge, challengin' me to come on or stand. I heaved boulders at the brute, as I calculated my gun would never pierce his armor no more 'n peas against armor plate. 'Twas what the black fellers call the 'prenty.' He lashed his ridgy tale, curved his back like the furriers in an old English meddler at home, and came a springin' t'rds me. He was a-roarin' like a lion and a-barkin' like a dog. I made tracks for me life, pronto, and lost no time in puttin' a hill atween me and that bird."

Mr. Blakeley measured the tracks of the "prenty" next day, and from one outside claw to the other found the distance was six feet three inches. All one may say is that in such an evolutionary lumber-room as Australia, there is nothing inherently improbable in the present existence of great saurians of the dinosaur type. Why, in one corner of southeastern Australia, in 1929, an earthworm longer than a man was found. He proved to be nine feet long. These worms make loud gurgling sounds and lay greenish translucent eggs three inches long.

UFOs Attack Earth ... The Out of Control Universe of Harold T. Wilkins

Monstrous and Strange They Are

Wilkins seems to have held a morbid fascination for the darker side of nature. His beasts are not "warm and fuzzy" like in a Steven Spielberg movie, but are instead fierce and prey on human flesh. His descriptions of man-eating abominable snowmen, Chinese dragons, a bird with the head of a monkey, as well as other bizarre monstrosities, conjure up our worst nightmares. These are not stories we will want to read before we retire, for they are certain to stir something in our subconscious that is more than capable of keeping us up all night! These are critters and creatures that roam the astral planes, even if they are not truly part of our physical realm. Nonetheless, Wilkins keeps us guessing as to how much of this we should believe in. Is it all a fantastic fantasy, or is it frighteningly genuine? Only the passage of time can indicate where the line can be drawn. At least Harold T. Wilkins knew we inevitably must face the unknown at some time in our lives, as these stories told by him in his "monsters monograph" illustrate.

THE "ABOMINABLE SNOWMAN" OF THE HIMALAYAS

The fastnesses of old Mother Asia have their tales of monsters and missing links. Uncle Sam's G.I.s who were in Burma, in the war, will recall, if they were anywhere near the "mystery river," called the Salween, whose upper reaches cut the Burma road, on the borders of the Chinese province of Yunnan, the stories of an ogre called by both Tibetans and Chinese, "the Abominable Snowman." He is said to be a gigantic, white, furry sort of anthropoid who, when lacking food, pounces down from the heights of the Himalayas and kills and eats men. Officers of the former British Indian army state they have seen this "Snowman" on the edge of the woods, high up in the Himalayas, and he seems to have been the subject of legends or stories all over India for centuries past. So far, the only clues to his existence have been footprints, human in shape, found high up on snow-clad mountains.

Mr. F.S. Smythe, member of the 1933 and 1936 expeditions seeking to climb the world's highest peak, Mt. Everest, stated at Bombay, in October, 1937, that he had been startled to, on the slopes of this mountain, by finding in the deep snow humanlike footprints nine inches wide and many feet apart, as if the monster progressed by great leaps. He had never seen anything like them, and his native porters called them "footprints of the Abominable Snowman." He photographed the tracks and sent pictures of them to London. For several days he followed these tracks, but never caught up with the mysterious creature who made them. His theory was that they might be the prints of some sort of giant bear, much bigger than a grizzly.

In the year before, Mr. Eric Shipton, an Everest climber, also said in Bombay that he had seen, 16,000 feet up on the giant mountain, tracks like elephant tracks, but resembling those of a biped, as the stride was long. His porters were terrified and said they had never seen the "Abominable Snowman," but had seen the bones of men devoured by him.

Colonel Howard Bury, leader of the first Everest expedition, said he saw prints of naked feet 20,000 feet up the mountain, in the snow. Then in 1938, Bhutanese coolies came back with news that they had seen the Snowmen themselves, on the 21,000-foot peak, Manas Saraban. They were so scared that they abandoned their trip to the summit. The Maharajah of Bhutan was so impressed with their air of veracity that he organized an expedition to track down the Snowmen with cameras. German mountaineers have also given similar testimony about these mysterious tracks in the snow.

They have been called nonsense by able scientists in London. Other theories are that they are prints of a Himalayan bear called the red bear, whose hind feet leave tracks like that of human feet, and have a stride of a yard; missing links in the chain of man's evolution who have black faces, silvery coverings of thick hair, perfect white teeth; Tarzans who speak with clucks and leap like the father of all monkeys from branch to branch in the Himalayas; and langurs, five feet tall monkeys who live at high altitudes in the Himalayas. But it is safer to say that the mystery of these "Abominable Snowmen" remains to be solved by the capture of one of them. No white man, at least, has yet made an authentic report of having seen them. Here, as in other matters, the open mind is best.

CHINESE "DRAGONS IN THE SLIME"

The Chinese used to be firm believers in the existence of dragons in the slime. In August, 1934, much excitement was caused by the discovery of the skeleton of a strange monster lying in the reeds of Lake Po Yanghu, near the city of Newchang, Central China. The spinal column of the monster was 18 feet long and he had 21 vertebrae and the same number of short ribs. His skull was domed and long and jointed, and from it protruded two horns some feet long. He was also fitted with a rudder-like tail. In the same year, stories of weird encounters with strange living monsters, who are said to be bulletproof, drifted from the jungles of Yunnan, western China, from a location between the rivers Mekong and the Kiu-sha, or upper Yangtzekiang. The story was told by an American missionary, Rev. Harold Young, when he arrived at Los Angeles, California. He told a rare yarn, calculated to tickle the newspaper boys:

"I was born in the Chinese village of Mong Lam, and the natives there have stories of creatures called 'Taws,' who are said to be shaggy, with silvery coats, and who loot native graveyards at night, while they are never seen by day. I have met these horrid beasts and found them to be apelike animals which neither bullets nor Chinese knives can kill."

To say truth, reverend, these Taws of yours look like a cross between the "Abominable Snowman" and the vampires and ghouls of the benighted Balkans of southeast Europe, or, as they used to be, of medieval England. They seem to have rather "high" tastes in 'ossflesh, too!

A BIRD WITH THE HEAD OF A MONKEY; A SPIDER WITH THE HEAD OF A MAN

Again, in September, 1934, a rich Chinese said he found in his house at Chumatien, in the province of Honan, a spider with a human face and small body, but abnormally large head. Its face was dead white, with black eyebrows, black nose, and horribly white lips. Its feet were dark brown. The arachnid—for, of course, spiders are not insects, being of the same species as the scorpion—was sent to the Chinese People's Educational Institute. Three years later, someone in Hangkow thought he captured a bird with the head of a monkey. He measured three feet in height, and eight feet in breadth, while the bird had "furry black feathers," four toes on each foot, and a mouth shaped like the bill of an eagle. This pet, suitable for an old battleaxe who had outlived a dozen husbands, must certainly be unique in the annals of ornithology.

A MISSING LINK BETWEEN REPTILE AND MAMMAL

Another reminder of the monstrous dinosaurs of North America came in September, 1938, when Dr. Lauge Koch, chief of the Danish Arctic Expedition, returned from East Greenland with the skeleton of a remarkable and unknown monster found lying in the mountains of Jameson Land, near Scoresby Sound. The finder was the geologist of the expedition, M. Stauber. The skeleton had mammalian characteristics, but seemed to be of the same age as the dinosaurs. The monster, therefore, may be on the vague borderline of transition between reptilia and mammals. The skeleton is now in Copenhagen Museum, Denmark.

PREHISTORIC ATOM BOMB OR BALKAN BUNYIP?

Old Europe, not to be behindhand in the discovery of monsters, discovered something which purported to be of the what-on-earth-is-it species. It may be recalled that, at the beginning of the 18th century of prose and reason, old Sir Isaac Newton paid for the publication of a book by Professor of mathematics and physics Scheuchzer of Zurich, Switzerland, who ought to have been a pretty hardheaded sort of chap. He assembled the testimony of many people in the Swiss Alps who swore they had met dragons high up there, though Scheuchzer had never had the luck to meet a dragon himself. He even included prints, and the book was dedicated to the august Royal Society of England. But before I cite story which ran the rounds of the newspapers of Paris, France, in March, 1929, I may give an extract from a curious and mystifying letter which appeared in an English annual of the year 1769:

UFOs Attack Earth . . . The Out of Control Universe of Harold T. Wilkins

"Letters from Paris give a surprising account from Amiens of a man and his wife and four horses being killed as they were at work in the harvest field, by something that came up out of the ground, and of which no trace was found; but only the smoking hole whence it issued. Two or three other people were struck down but not much hurt. The surgeons who inspected the bones of those who were killed did not discover the least wound, but only a considerable swelling and great deformity of features. The woman, who is young and handsome, appeared a shocking spectacle."

Any theory may fit in with this mysterious affair, from a prehistoric atom bomb to a Balkan bunyip, and your idea, reader, is as good as mine.

Now, here is the Paris newspaper story of March, 1929. It would appear that the very father of dragons appeared in the remote countryside round the village of Villesang, in the Puy de Dome, which is located in the mountainous country of the Auvergne, in west central Europe:

"The people here are living in terror of an alleged supernatural monster which, like the Grendel of Beowulf, lurks at the bottom of a large lake. After nightfall, there issues from the dark lake awe-inspiring sounds as from some monstrous giant of a beast. Those who hear the noises say they resemble nothing on earth ever heard before. Fires have been it round the lake. Men issue forth every half hour and fire shots in the direction of the diabolical uproar, but the sounds still continue without abatement. Some local people recall a legend about a fabulous beast which took toll of local folk—a kind of Dragon of Wantley or Minotaur of Crete. They hold the firm belief that a monster of this sort is raising hell in the lake after nightfall."

Well, reader, I trust these stories of mine have given you some entertainment.

UFOs Attack Earth . . . The Out of Control Universe of Harold T. Wilkins

Bat-Like Creature Seen Over California

Moving forward in his career, Harold T. Wilkins began to center his attention on the UFO phenomenon as the unknown objects started to appear all over the planet, capturing the imagination of a civilization that was itself just starting to dream about conquering space and encountering inhabited worlds. Wilkins is determined to make sense out of what is being seen, and in the process he creates myths and blazes new trails among the stars.

In this chapter, we begin to examine some of the UFO stories that Harold T. Wilkins collected, beginning with his book *Flying Saucers On The Attack*, first published in 1954. The story here concerns a UFO that appeared to be not a simple machine aircraft, but a living creature with bat-like wings, a phenomenon perhaps more animal than technological. Wilkins quotes several witnesses from the Southern California area who saw the strange bat craft in 1946, some months before Kenneth Arnold's sighting the next year, which is often said to begin the modern UFO era. The stories told here also smack eerily of the Mothman sightings that would come nearly two decades later and which the legendary researcher John Keel has covered thoroughly in his own writings.

⚜ ⚜ ⚜

In 1946, the phenomena, whatever they were and are, did not always take the form of balls, orange lights, or glowing spheres, but that of a very strange object "with wings," described by one witness as looking like a "huge bat." It appeared high in the sky over San Diego, California, between 7:25 P.M. and 9 P.M. on October 9, 1946. At the time, many people were out on rooftops and the top floors of skyscrapers, watching a shower of meteors. I have reports from sixteen people in San Diego who say they saw this queer object, and who, not unnaturally, would be most indignant if you suggested that they were suffering from hallucinations or mass-hysteria, or had misinterpreted some natural and astronomical phenomena, like meteorites, the moon or the planet Venus.

These eyewitnesses number seven men, eight women, and a youth. Seven of these eyewitnesses say that the mysterious object had wings. They say it crossed the moon's disk, looked like an extremely long plane, carrying two reddish lights, and traveled at an amazing speed. It was bluish-white in color.

One woman, whose name and address I have, said, "The strange object was certainly no airplane. The wings, which moved, were too wide for any bird. Indeed, they were rather like the wings of a butterfly. The whole object emitted a red glow."

Another woman and a man say the object looked like a bat, hooked, weird and very large. One woman saw it from between two houses, and it took at least 80 seconds to cross that space; so that, at that time, "it must have changed speed from very fast to slow." Two other witnesses who saw the same weird object from different parts of Southern California say it was stationary for some time. "Then it moved slowly, accelerated and left a trail of luminosity behind it. At that time its motion was very slow." A woman, who is a professional astronomer, took a time exposure of the moon, and says that the film, when developed, showed a strange effect of smoke rings or halations seen on films and plates, as if fire were coming out of the moon, or as if a passing object had left a vapor trail.

The sum total of the eyewitnesses' evidence is that this strange object, which had the appearance of a spaceship, remained far overhead all night, considerably varied its rate of speed, and was alternately brilliantly illuminated and dark. There was also an occasional emission of a flash of light, or a luminous jet of glasses.

MORE COMPARISONS TO A LIVING CREATURE

Now, the statement of the bat-like appearance of this strange object seen high in the sky over San Diego, California, may be compared with the report made by a Dr. F.B. Harris in the 1912 issue of "Popular Astronomy": "In the evening of January 27, 1912, I saw an intensely black object, like a crow, poised upon the moon. I estimated it at 250 miles long by 50 miles wide. I cannot but think that a very interesting phenomenon happened."

I note, too, that Miss Ella Young, an American authoress, wrote to Mr. Meade Layne, M.A., who has devoted much time to the investigation of these remarkable phenomena, seen at various dates in the western and eastern states of the U.S.A., "I believe I saw a spaceship early in 1927, at the Casa Madrona Hotel, Sausalito (Marin County, California). I was, one morning, sitting outside the hotel, thinking of nothing in particular, when I saw a cigar-shaped craft shoot out of a cloud beyond the bay, and cross the sky toward Tamalpais. At first, I thought it must be a U.S. airship, but soon changed my mind. It was not shaped like the *Akron* (A well-known U.S. dirigible in the 1920s, Author's Note by Harold T. Wilkins). It was long and slender, of yellow color, and traveling at a great speed. As it came opposite me, it seemed to progress by alternately contracting and elongating its body.

EXTRATERRESTRIAL ANIMALS

One cannot, however, join the lady in her fascinating conjecture—albeit the Project Saucer of the U.S. Air Force says, humorously, that its experts have remotely considered "the possible existence of some strange extraterrestrial animals, since many of the flying saucer objects described (as seen over American territory) acted more like animals than anything else"—that the strange skyship she saw came from a world fairly close to us, but invisible, and that "they have spirited away whole ships with their crews, and humans, and even dumped a whole cargo of sea serpents and prehistoric animals on our earth." This was the sort of thing so often said, with a wink in his sardonic eye, by the late Charles Fort. In relation to mysteries like that of the **Mary Celeste**, he seemed to enjoy "guying" his true believers, as apparently, he deemed that one true believer was worse than ten prophets.

She further adds what is undoubtedly a repetition of other quite true observations made by people in Europe and America, both before and long after 1927: "In October 1946, I saw a most brilliant light break out in the sky, soon after sundown. It lasted a few seconds and was not a meteor, nor came from a burning plane. Nothing then fell towards the Earth." A friend was with her, she adds, when, on December 30, 1946, "We were on high ground that curves southward from Morrow Bay. The sun had just gone down, and the time was 5:35 P.M., when suddenly, a dark object appeared in the sky. It came forward and grew more distinct. On the golden sky it looked very black. It came forward, head-on, and had a bat-like appearance, owing to the curvature of its wings. I am not sure if there were motions at the extreme tip of the wings; but the strange machine seemed to stand still for several minutes and its form was very distinct. Suddenly it either lowered itself toward the horizon, or the bank of cloud-mist made an upward movement—maybe both movements occurred—for the machine passed behind the cloud and did not reappear. Immediately afterwards, a great flush of color spread over the sea."

The woman with Miss Young, at this time, corroborated the statement that the strange machine hung poised in the air for more than five minutes, and had wings curved like those of a bat.

THE PSYCHIC VERSION OF EVENTS

What was the mysterious object that hung all night in the sky over San Diego? Was it a spaceship? Some of the eyewitnesses thought the machine was being navigated, but not in the manner of an airplane. Mr. Mark Probert, who was in company with a youth named Fernando Esevano, when the weird bat-like, winged machine stood high in the sky over San Diego, on the night of October 9, 1946, volunteers a statement which he apparently obtained from some psychic or clairaudient source, in California. The "source" says the machine comes from "some planet west of the moon"—but how, in outer space, can one orient a planet and speak of spatial points? This is a difficulty of orientation—one of the perplexing problems, by the way, that will, in the years ahead, confront navigators of some type of rocket, or atomic-power-driven spaceship, when it quits the Earth on a voyage to Mars or Venus or Jupiter.

Mr. Probert tells us, "The strange machine is called the **Kareeta**, or the **Corida**. It is attracted at this time because the Earth is emitting a column of light, which makes it easier of approach. The machine is powered by people possessing a very advanced knowledge of antigravity forces. It has 10,000 parts, a small but very powerful motor operating by electricity, and moving the wings, and an outer structure of light balsam wood, coated with an alloy. The people are non-aggressive and have been trying to contact the Earth for many years. They have very light bodies. They fear to land, but would be willing to meet a committee of scientists at an isolated spot, or on a mountaintop."

Again, I presume to offer no comment on the above, or on the unknown place of origin of this queer winged craft, vaguely said to come from "some world west of the moon."

UFOs Attack Earth . . . The Out of Control Universe of Harold T. Wilkins

The Martian Cat Among The Pigeons

Harold T. Wilkins states categorically in the opening paragraphs of this next chapter from *Flying Saucers On The Attack* that it is foolish to make the assumption that all of the flying saucer occupants are somehow kindly and benevolent. He then goes on to catalog numerous sighting reports from that pivotal year of 1947, including a brief mention of the Roswell Incident and the use of weather balloons as a cover story by the military. He was also one of the first to grapple with the idea that that early wave of UFO sightings may have had a great deal to do with mankind's discovery of nuclear weapons and a race of aliens who sought to keep that terrifying new power under control for their own sake. Along the way, he relates the case of a truck driver frightened out of his wits by a silver sphere in the sky and a bridge in Oregon whose steel parts were literally melted away in what Wilkins feels may have been a kind of "friendly warning" from H.G. Wells-type Martians. All in all, a very interesting grab bag of Wilkins at his most fascinating. By the way, all the italics herein are Wilkins' own.

⚜ ⚜ ⚜

In certain mystical and pseudo-mystical circles, both in the U.S.A. and Canada, and to a lesser extent in Great Britain, there is being foolishly propagated an illusion that *all* the mysterious and elusive entities of the flying saucers, coming whence no one really *knows*, are benevolent super-beings, radiating an unearthly great love and understanding, "like a warm embrace, with wisdom," that have made a number of gentlemen yearn to follow them, and any "golden-haired man onboard Venusian satellite disks, and more beautiful than a woman," even into Via Galactea, though he might never return from these abodes of cosmic bliss.

This is a dangerous illusion! A pipe—or opium—dream.

It may be true that, so far as has yet appeared, *some* of these cosmic visitants are non-aggressive, and merely exploratory, like Cook's Cosmic Tourists having a look over our planet. BUT—there are others! And, here and there in this book, I shall cite reports of strange and disturbing incidents, not merely in the U.S., but in Great Britain, that convey the unpleasant impression that some of these entities—and I have in mind, particularly, a weird unidentified object of cigar-shape held stationary in the center of a rapidly rotating ring, like Saturn in *his rings*—appear unmistakably hostile to this planet of ours, and show reactions that can by no means be regarded as fear-reactions.

There are saucers, not manned by "little men," or captained by women, but by entities no one knows or has ever seen, who irresponsible behavior takes the form of arson on quite a large and dangerous scale. They seem to have heat ray projectors recalling those of H.G. Wells' **Men From Mars**, all brains and now bowels, and command of powers conferred by a very advanced science. I may again remind some of the sentimental idealists, who write on this aspect of a new and amazing age, that it does not follow that this planet of ours, which has seen two insane world wars in less than one man's lifetime, necessarily rolls on its solar way in the midst only of other worlds that are friendly to it. Some morning stars may *not* be singing for joy! In this book, my purpose is not to disseminate mystic nonsense and soothing syrup, like some female writer telling the world, for the twentieth time, about the loves of an old priest of Chaldea, or a young and lovely priestess of Atlantis, and lying on a carpet before a roaring coal fire, in some West End drawing room displaying her own scanty-skirted charms, to be photographed for the benefit of free advertisement of her new novel, in the columns of a bright morning newspaper.

What appears like unpleasant truth should be told, so far as one may know it, to men and women of courage and intelligence.

THE SAUCERS HAVE A BUSY SUMMER

Towards the end of the summer of 1947, there were reports that eight mysterious flying saucers had been seen landing in the clearings of a forest of a mountainside, near St. Marie, Idaho. It was said to have happened in the broad light of day, and a woman, who said she had seen them landing, was mystified, because she could not see them after they landed! "They were like washing tubs, and the size of a five-roomed house." A Roman Catholic priest at Grafton, Wisconsin, heard a whirring and swishing sound, followed by a thud and a mild explosion in his parish yard. He found a sheet-metal disk, some 18 inches long,

UFOs Attack Earth . . . The Out of Control Universe of Harold T. Wilkins

like a circular saw blade. It was warm to the touch and weighed five pounds. A hole was in the middle of the disk, and in its opening were "gadgets and some wires." Whether this was what Project Saucer might call a prankster's hoax, I am unable to say. The incident was like the case reported, about the same time, by a tobacco wholesaler, Lloyd Bennet, at Oelwein, Iowa. He said no planes were overhead, when an object, shaped like a piece of metal, six and one-half inches wide and one-eighth of an inch thick, "swished through the trees and landed" on his lawn.

U.S. military planes on patrol with photo equipment over the Pacific coast at this time, November 1947, had no luck, despite sightings of saucers reported from thirty states of U.S. Yet, in Western Ontario, Canada, many people said they saw *two large formations* of strange disks moving across the sky in a wide arc. These disks were said to have varied in size, from an apparent eight inches to that of a large, five-roomed house!

Mass hallucination, mass hysteria, and faulty observations do *not* seem to explain the queer phenomena seen, at this time, in Sweden. According to the newspaper, the Stockholm **Aftonbladet**, a flying saucer was seen over Stockholm late on a Sunday night. On that very day, July 7, 1947, a professor of physiology at Sydney University, N.S.W., Australia, told his pupils that flying saucers were "merely illusions created by the red corpuscles passing in front of the retina of the eye, when one stood still and gazed at a fixed point in the sky." Just "spots in the eye!" But that did not seem to be the explanation for what a man, at this very time, saw at Brighton, Sussex, England. He and his wife were on the beach at 4 P.M., when he saw "something like the moon, only bigger, fly over Black Rock cliffs and out to sea."

Chile now had a turn at the sightings of "spots in the eye." A strange object appeared, slowly moving through the sky and discharging white gases. It was seen by scientists at Del Salto Observatory, who said that this "singular meteor" remained visible for a certain time, crossing the horizon at 3,000 miles an hour. So it could *not* have been a meteor, to have been visible for "a certain time"! The observatory asked 300 observers in the southern hemisphere to be on the alert, and this was just at the time when reports of saucers came from other parts of Chile, Japan, and Holland, and when many people in Naples, Italy, said they had seen "a shining disk" fly *slowly* across the sky from east to west, in the night.

UFOs Attack Earth... The Out of Control Universe of Harold T. Wilkins

WILKINS' EARLY REPORT ON ROSWELL

Close to the place where the first atomic bomb was tested, a rancher at Roswell, New Mexico, was said, in July 1947, to have found a flying saucer. It landed in his ranch, and was inspected by officers of the 509th Atomic Bomber group of the 8th U.S. Air Force, who sent it to a "higher quarter." This reported find followed a report from Dr. C.J. Zohn, guided missile expert of the U.S. Naval Laboratory, that he and two other scientists had sighted a flying saucer near White Sands, a proving ground to which public access is prohibited, in New Mexico. Down came U.S. Army authorities who declared this was merely a weather balloon; despite the plain statement of Mr. Ivan B. Tannehill, weather bureau chief forecaster, that it was unlikely that this mysterious object, speeding through the skies at a speed above the rate of transmission of sound waves, could have been a weather balloon. He pointed out that weather balloons have been in use for many years.

At this juncture, when the U.S. Air and Army authorities were talking of balloons, a baffling incident happened, on July 8, 1947, at one of the United States' most secret air bases, that at Muroc, California, where the latest supersonic aircraft were located. At 9:20 P.M., Lieut. J. C. McHenry saw two silver objects, spherical in shape, moving at 300 miles an hour at a height of 8,000 feet. Three other men at the same airport saw them. These objects were *traveling against the wind*, and so were neither weather nor cosmic ray balloons. Earlier the same day, two military engineers had seen a metallic disk diving and oscillating for ten minutes over Muroc Airfield! It would seem that the entities were particularly interested in Muroc Airfield secrets. It is curious that no plane took off from the ground to try to intercept them—curious, since, as I say, *orders had been issued for that very purpose.*

Indeed it would seem as if these mysterious disks had a particular interest, in June-July 1947, in Oregon, Washington, California, and ranging a good way inland from the Pacific coast. Some might have said that they were machines of terrestrial origin engaged in mapping these regions of the U.S.A. But this theory would not fit in with the great speed of these machines—far above that of sound-transmission. Also, while some of the disks seemed under intelligent, *direct control*, others, of different shape and size, had the air of being remotely controlled!

ENCOUNTER WITH A BLINDING LIGHT

For example there was the silver ball seen at 4 P.M. on July 30, 1947, by John E. Ostrom of Nissa, Oregon. He is a 68-year-old man and was, on that day, driving a motor truck along a road near Tamarack, Idaho. He was doing about 45 miles an hour, when, on a sudden, he was startled by a blinding light overhead. Looking up, he saw, with terror and amazement, a silver ball of blinding brilliance slanting down from the sky! It was coming at an angle of 30 degrees, and straight towards his truck. Instinctively, he let go the steering wheel, and cowered down, covering his face with his hands. He felt it must hit his vehicle. It did! It hit the top of his truck and glanced off. Ostrom recovered himself, stopped the engine, and got out. He saw a phenomenon.

Where the ball had hit the truck was a scorched spot the size of a silver dollar. *It had melted the metal and left no hole.* What was peculiar was that, instead of a perforation, as would normally have happened, the scorched spot showed *what looked like a welding* in the original metal of the truck! According to a Seattle newspaper clipping I have, expert welders, who subsequently examined the patch, positively affirmed that something must have welded that part of the truck. Mr. Ostrom, however, most emphatically states that no repair or welding had ever been done to the top or cab of his truck, and that the singular effect had been produced by the contact of the silver ball. The newspaper adds that there are traces, on that part of the truck, of molten metal *which seems* to have been abraded from the surface of the silver ball which hit the truck. Why has this abrasion not been chemically and metallurgiclly examined or analyzed?

Was *this* a meteor?

At first sight, the answer might be *yes*. But it happens that, in this very region where Ostrom had his adventure, forest fires of a mysterious origin were reported by rangers in this very summer of 1947. And yet, no meteoric shower was reported over the Cascades at the time. The mystery deepened when another queer thing happened. A Wellsian, Martian phenomenon!

UFOs Attack Earth ... The Out of Control Universe of Harold T. Wilkins

A FRIENDLY WARNING FROM MARS?

Six days before Mr. Ostrom had his adventure with the silver ball, a man named Bowman, with his wife and niece, were driving along a road towards a part-suspension, part-trestle bridge that spans the Salmon River, in Oregon. The bridge is about 420 feet long, and spans a canon some 85 feet deep. The Bowmans found that the bridge was aflame from end to end. They halted the car and took photos, for they had cameras with them. Now, a very peculiar feature about this fire struck Mr. Bowman. The day was sunny, no could was in the sky, and there was no thunder or lightning. Yet, not only *one* part of the bridge was on fire. *The whole bridge had been simultaneously set afire*! Oregon road engineers came on the scene and investigated. They found that the steel cables of the bridge had been *melted*. Now, the melting point of steel is more than 2,000 degrees Fahrenheit.

I here put a question: Had some heat ray from some mysterious cosmic machine, reminiscent of the heat ray of the Martians in H.G. Wells' well known novel, been projected onto the Salmon River gorge by unseen enemies, controlling some radiator in one of the nine immense and unknown machines seen by Arnold, in that very summer of 1947? If the answer to this very disquieting question be *yes*, then, what may happen, in some time to come, to accumulating stockpiles of hydrogen and super-atomic bombs—the hydrogen bomb of which two, simultaneously exploding, can, says a famous nuclear physicist, set the earth off her orbit? I do *not* say that these would be mysteriously exploded, if lunatic terrestrial powers were about to arrange to toss them at each other, but that there might be other unknown ways of deactivation. For consider, *if* there be other inhabited worlds, we share with *them* the solar cosmos, and *they* may not choose to remain inert and hover around while lunatics blast out into space from this Earth's orbit terribly dangerous and uncontrollable radio-activities, which may affect other worlds and the central sun. If politicians, masquerading as statesmen, pay no heed to warnings, perhaps the priests of science may, for their own safety, ponder and refrain before it be too late!

Local Oregon forest rangers say that it would have been impossible that burning wood trestles, in this bridge, could have generated a furnace heat capable of melting steel, as did this strange fire. The mystery has never been cleared up. But if that fire were a "demonstration" from mysterious flying saucers, can it be said that it may be deemed not a token of hostile intent, but a *warning to those who have brains to consider*?

MAKING SENSE OF THE UNKNOWABLE

What is so strange is that these weird visible, and then alternately invisible machines seem to be linked with mysterious bodies that are both vertiginously fast, and then remarkably slow bodies, shaped like cones, cigars, sausages, torpedoes, of blue, green, red, yellow and blazing, which can roar, flash, or explode in the air, and have been called flying saucers. They may, or may not be, satellites under the control of some unseen mother-ship of fantastic size. Or, again, more than one entity is, or may be, involved, and more than one extraterrestrial world may be visiting our skies!

We cannot yet say! All we can say is that these weird things are not meteors or comets. They range from the fantastic size of *half a mile, or even more*, to that of a 55-feet long airliner, and much smaller disks. There are even vast, golden-hued spheres, *a mile in diameter*, tracked by radar, as flying in the stratosphere! It has to be believed, or not. It would also seem that these bodies emanate from vastly different worlds than ours, some of them apparently of a very different order of wave length, whose analogy is that of the invisible rays in the solar spectrum contrasted with the visible octaves at the red or blue end, or sound waves, perceptible to normal human hearing, as compared with ultrasonic waves perceptible by some animals or birds, but not by human beings. On the other hand, it would appear that some of these mysterious bodies may come from worlds as tangible and material as our own, and likely to be populated with beings like ourselves—that is, visible in what we may call "normal" conditions!

Tales Of An Alien Death Ray And Explosions In The Sky

Harold T. Wilkins continues his tirade against what he felt was the somewhat sappy contention that all UFOs carried inside them benevolent space brothers. In the following story excerpts, he gives a detailed account of the famous Captain Thomas F. Mantell story, a pilot whose plane crashed as he pursued a UFO through the skies over Fort Knox, Kentucky. Wilkins says he has some information about the Mantell incident not included in the public reports of the time. He also offers a lively history of an explosion that took place in the skies over Kansas in 1948, one of the classic stories in the Fortean mode that Wilkins collected, but with decidedly extraterrestrial overtones.

RIPPED FROM THE SKIES ABOVE

In the previous chapter, I emphasized the folly of theories that *all* flying saucers are inoffensive. Now, we pass from the stages in which bridges and forests are set on fire by mysterious non-terrestrial entities aloft in our skies—or perhaps even out in space—to a dramatic adventure in which a fine U.S. pilot lost his life. The story has been given in other saucer books; but strange and mysterious phases, here recorded, have *not* been given, and are very little known outside the camaraderie of American Air Force pilots who dare not tell all the know.

It was on January 7, 1948, that Captain Thos. F. Mantell, a Kentucky Air pilot of the National Guard, with a first class record in the second World War, was ordered, with two other pilots then in the air, to give chase to a strange, unidentified object, looking like an ice cream cone with a tip of red, which had been seen hovering high in the air over the air base at Godman, near Fort Knox, Kentucky. It may be recalled that, at Fort Knox, is or was stored the immense hoard of gold accumulated by the U.S.A. from the munitions debtors, principally Great Britain in the first world war.

Mantell was in the air, and the orders came from the commandant of the Godman Air Base, Colonel Guy F. Hix, who, in growing excitement, had for some time been watching through binoculars, from the top of the air tower, the curious antics of this mysterious body. As the sun glanced on it, the body gleamed like burnished silver.

Colonel Hix said: "It was umbrella-shaped, half the apparent size of the moon, and white in color, except for a streamer of red which seemed to be rotating."

He had been watching the mysterious thing for two hours, so that it is obvious that the region had some strong attraction for the entities, whoever, or whatever they were. It might be that they had instruments which reacted strongly from radiations thrown out by the vast gold vaults below—instruments which, despite yarns to the contrary, no terrestrial treasure hunter possesses at this time! However, that is merely conjecture.

Three of the pilots tried to close in on the thing, and reported on their radio telephone back to the Godman air tower, that the "size of this thing is *tremendous!*" One pilot said it looked like a tear drop, and at times seemed almost fluid! Then the flight leader, Mantell, came in on the air, with his radio report:

"The object is traveling at half my speed, and 12 o'clock high. I'm going to close in right now, for a good look. It's directly ahead of me. The thing looks metallic and of *tremendous size*. It's going up now and forward as fast as I am. That's 360 miles an hour. I'm going up to 20,000 feet, and if I'm no closer, I'll abandon chase."

The time was 3:15 P.M. It is said to have been the last radio contact made by Mantell, with Godman air base tower; but I have to say that an observer, on that airfield, told me that not *all* the report made by Mantell has been revealed by the Saucer Project.

The two other pilots radioed back that the thing was still far above them, and the planes had reached a ceiling of 20,000 feet. They added: "This strange object is too high for us to catch. It's going too fast."

At this time, Colonel Hix, his executive officer, Lieut. Col. Garrison Wood, and other officers were watching this flying saucer through 8-power binoculars. Said Hix: "I can't account for the fact that this celestial body—as I think it is—*did not move as we looked at it*. I don't know what it was."

MANTELL CONTINUES TO GIVE CHASE

Now came a radio from the two other pilots that the object had vanished into cloud at a *terrific speed*. They broke off pursuit, but Mantell went on climbing. He must have been well over 20,000 feet, when he radioed back—this does *not* occur in the official report of Project Saucer: "Am not gaining on it. I shall have to break off the chase soon."

It is believed that Mantell also added some remarkable details about the fantastic speed, the tremendous size, and the appearance of the weird object, and I am told that not even Mantell's widow was given *all* his last message. A few seconds after this last message, something happened! His machine was seen to explode in midair. A Mr. Glen Moyes, who saw the crash, said that Mantell's plane—a first class machine, P.51—went into a dive, at 20,000 feet, and began to disintegrate when about half that height above the ground. But, a woman on whose farm poor Mantell's plane crashed, said she had heard it roar over her house and then saw it fall apart at treetop height. All accounts, however, agree that Mantell was instantaneously killed.

[Author's note from Harold T. Wilkins: I am asked, by a mechanical engineer living at Cuyahoga Falls, Ohio, to note that a P.51, flown by Captain Mantell, does not crash when the pilot drops the controls. It glides. He also points out that a crashed plane does not spread wreckage over an area of half a mile, as did Mantell's P.51. The inference, therefore, is that Mantell's plane met something far more mysterious than a crash, or a glide, resulting from an alleged dropping of controls. Moreover, Mantell, as a pilot in World War II, knew well the signs of oxygen deficiency, resulting in a blackout at a high altitude. Again, something more than a mere blackout occurred.]

WAS A DEATH RAY RESPONSIBLE?

UFOs Attack Earth . . . The Out of Control Universe of Harold T. Wilkins

Some may say—and the present author is impenitently among them!—that some lethal ray of immense power and unknown type had been directed at Mantell and his plane by the entities in the weird and vast machine, who may have deemed that they were going to be attacked, or wished to demonstrate to terrestrial military power, with its antiaircraft batteries, the folly of any close approach. It reminds us of the heat ray directed by the Men from Mars in the late H.G. Wells' novel, against the British Army embattled in Surrey, with heavy artillery, and the British battleships in the English Channel and Straits of Dover, when the fantastically stilted walking machines of the Martians advanced from about Margrate across the sea towards the British Navy. In this case, it will be recalled, a monitor-ram fused under the tremendous blast of Martian heat rays and exploded in live steam and flames.

But one thing must be emphasized: Mantell was a man with a fine record, level-headed and certainly not a man to have given chase to the planet Venus—actually at the time invisible in the sky!—or to have rashly persisted until blackout and loss of oxygen, with suffocation.

An amazing circumstance must here be recorded: Colonel Hix and another officer had sighted the strange machine, *for hours*, along an upright staff used as a "fix," *when, all that time, it remained motionless*, as not even a helicopter would, or could do.

On the day of the crash, about 5 P.M., came a report from an airfield at Columbus, Ohio, that a glowing disk was seen hurtling across the sky at an estimated speed of 550 miles an hour. It was white and orange, and emitted an exhaust some five times its own length. This was at Lockbourne air base, and the observers said the disk was followed from the observation tower for more than 20 minutes. It glowed from white to amber, appeared round or oval, and traveled in level flight. At one time it seemed to "motion like an elevator," and then appeared "to touch the ground." No sound was heard from it, and it finally faded and lowered towards the horizon. At the Clinton County Army Air Base, at Wilmington, Ohio, observers reported: "A flaming red cone trailing a gaseous green mist tore through the sky at 7:55 P.M."

This apparition looks very much like the machine that, over four hours earlier, smashed Mantell and his plane, or, if not, it was one of the same type. At the same control tower, a staff sergeant and corporal saw the "red cone maneuvering for 35 minutes, when it seemed to vanish over the horizon." They added: "It seemed to hang suspended in the air at intervals. Then it came down.

It then ascended at what looked like a terrific speed. The intense brightness from this phenomenon in the sky pierced through a heavy cloud layer which intermittently passed over the region." It is to be noted that thousands of people witnessed this phenomenon.

THE SKY EXPLODES OVER KANSAS

On February 18, 1948, a terrific explosion in the sky over Kansas rocked buildings, broke windows, and did damage over a wide area in Kansas, Nebraska, and Oklahoma. On that day, a ball of fire exploded over Nortons, Kansas, and a blue-white cloud, the result of the explosion, was visible for hours and was photographed. I have a copy of the photograph. The explosion was so abnormal that it was seen in six states: Kansas, Texas, New Mexico, Oklahoma, Nebraska and Colorado. The authorities at Chamberlain Observatory, University of Denver, were positive that it was no meteor, and they knew of no astronomical phenomena that explained it. This strange sphere of fire was seen over two towns in Oklahoma, and its speed was reckoned at 600 miles an hour, too slow for a meteor, which moves in miles a second. There was, first, the terrific blast of an explosion that shook buildings with the force of an earthquake. The blast was followed a roar of appalling character that last ten seconds. Then there appeared, at what was calculated to be 35 miles high in the sky, a strange blue cloud that rolled and bellied forth like a monstrous dragon *in etremis*! Two hours later, there appeared a B-29 bomber which circled around the area of the cloud till sunset.

There is, however, no confirmation of the reports of two other B-29 pilots that, before the appalling explosion, that they had seen a long, cylindrical, shining metal projectile with a shiny nose, and a terrific burst of flame at its rear end. This amazing projectile was said to have had the prodigious length of ten miles and to have traveled at 1,800 miles an hour! Truly, an incredible story! Oddly enough, between the two blasts, very high in the sky, a streak of smoke punctuated by a jelly roll of gases, or steam, which blossomed into another curious roll, suggested *rocket blasts*, but not from any terrestrial firing range. No; possibly from a *rocket-type* of mysterious spaceship of non-terrestrial origin!

Had some mysterious cosmic visitant met with a terrible accident?

Whatever this phenomenon was, there came reports that it traveled *erratically before the explosions*, and in a way no meteor would do. A pilot, flying at 12,500 feet, said that the explosion seemed to come from the ground. Yet no fragments were found on the ground! He was flying from Walla Walla when he saw a blue-green ball come across the nose of his plane, so near that he feared a crash. But the strange ball ascended straight on up and vanished. Twenty minutes later, when his plane was midway between Baker, Idaho, and La Grande, he saw another ball of blue fire, traveling *horizontally*. He said that in all the war years when he had traveled the Burma Road, he had never been so frightened, and he had been used to dangerous missions. At about this time, two other pilots in the air above Burley, Idaho—this state seems to hold some attraction for these amazing visitants!—saw a brilliant blue-green light traveling horizontally, with a bright sea-green tail. It was some four miles away. It very definitely shot up into space.

A FARMER GETS A CLOSER LOOK

Queer stories were associated with this portentous explosion of the mysterious blue object. A Stockton, Kansas, farmer said that just before the explosion, he saw a strange saucer wobbling over his home when it came within six feet of him.

"It stopped in the air, level with my face, and wobbled around for an instant with fire belching out, and then being sucked back in. It was about four feet long and shaped like a funnel. Sparks suddenly showered from it and the fire increased as if a fuse had been lit. It took off in a northwest direction, very fast, gaining altitude as it went. My wife came out and watched it fly off, leaving a trail of smoke. Suddenly, a great cloud of smoke appeared in the sky, and in a few seconds, we heard a terrible explosion. I could feel the heat from where the object came near the ground."

But was this the amazing projectile seen by the pilots of the B-29 planes? Surely not! They said it was of immense size. It may be that it had a satellite connection with the immense object, or even, as a Texas astronomer averred, was really an achondrite, or peculiar stone meteor. Anyway, it gave the Project Saucer experts a chance to align this small body with the immense one, and explain both as meteorites—which is an absurdity. In any event, unless the farmer and his wife were born and imaginative liars, even the achondrite showed very peculiar behavior for a meteorite!

UFOs Attack Earth... The Out of Control Universe of Harold T. Wilkins

Are The UFO Occupants Midgets?

Further on in *Flying Saucers On The Attack*, Harold T. Wilkins discusses the possible diminutive size of the UFO occupants, conjecturing that they may in fact be midgets. One must remember that this was in the early 1950s, long before reports of the standard gray aliens began to proliferate widely, starting in the mid-1960s with the Barney and Betty Hill abduction case and continuing through Whitley Strieber's landmark abduction history *Communion* and on into the present. Wilkins comes at this notion a little differently.

He theorizes that only an alien life form of something like a midget size could withstand the extreme gravitational forces involved in the saucers' seemingly impossible aerial maneuvers, carried out at incredible speeds that no human being could survive. Wilkins was writing at a time when it was still thought possible that the UFOs and their smallish occupants could be from Mars or Venus, which strikes us today as fanciful to say the least. But one can at least see the first trickles of the stream that would come to form our present vision of the gray aliens as shorter than human beings and capable of surviving aerial gymnastics far beyond our own abilities. Also included in this chapter are stories of possible alien attempts to communicate with humankind by radio, as well as the tale of an airliner that vanished just after sending a cryptic, possibly alien-controlled, message to the airport tower.

⚜ ⚜ ⚜

AT A MIND-BOGGLING SPEED

The day was Sunday, April 6, 1949, the sky bright and sunny, and as this is an arid region where rain may not fall even once a year, the air was crystalline. Scientists and U.S. Navy officers had sent up a weather balloon, northwest of the White Sands Proving Ground. Its upward flight was tracked by theodolites and a stopwatch. Of the five observers, one held the watch and another the telescope. The balloon was well aloft when the man with the telescope was startled. Swiveling his telescope around to the east, he watched a singular disk approaching the upward path of the balloon. As he did so, a scientist tracked the disk through a theodolite. The strange object appeared to be an ellipsoid, about 100 feet wide, and some 56 miles high. Seen from the rear end, its shape might have suggested a pointed cigar, with a saucer-shaped or convex surface.

Now, a ballistics expert calculated the speed of the disk. *It was five miles a second*! He must have gasped with astonishment. There has yet been devised no motor on earth that will power a machine to travel at this fantastic speed! That is, a speed of flight of *18,000 miles an hour*. And it must be realized that this mysterious discoidal machine, seen 56 miles high in the sky, was *not* a high trajectory rocket missile.

Then came another amazing incident.

The thing suddenly swerved upwards, *and in ten seconds* had increased its altitude above the earth *by 25 miles*. Again, mathematicians, astrophysicists, and ballistic experts calculated that the tremendous force exerted in this prodigious acceleration was equivalent to *twenty times the pull of the terrestrial gravity field*. No human being of our earth could endure such a terrific pull without having every cell in his body ruptured. The strange disk was in sight for about a minute.

The experts of the U.S. Air Force Project Saucer at the Wright-Patterson airfield at Dayton, Ohio, investigated this amazing affair, and were told by responsible eyewitnesses that this ellipsoidal disk was white, emitted no stream of light, and jetted out no exhaust or trail of vapor. But this was not the last amazing experience.

These strange machines put in another sensational appearance at the White Sands Proving Ground, New Mexico, on June 10, 1949. On that day, a high trajectory, stratospheric guided missile was being fired. As the missile roared upwards into the sunlit sky, observers were astonished. Two white balls suddenly appeared and lit out in pursuit of the missile, whose speed was then about 2097.3 feet a second, or approximately 1,430 miles an hour. Both balls shot through the exhaust trails of the rocket-missile, got ahead of it, and then joined each other well in front of the roaring rocket! They then ascended and vanished from sight. One of these balls was tracked by a Navy observation post, located on the Oregon Mountains, and seen to be speeding to the west. The observer at the time did not know what it was, but seems to have supposed that it was a high trajectory rocket that had got out of control and might crash on some city, with catastrophic effect.

It may also be noted that, on the say these vertiginous white balls were seen, high in the skies of New Mexico, the wind at an altitude of 20 miles in the sky was moving in a direction opposite to that taken by the ball seen from the Oregon Mountains observation post; so that the ball was moving at great speed *against a very strong wind*.

None can say whence these amazing balls came. To say Mars or Venus is to beg a very big question that cannot now be answered, in the present state of our astronomical knowledge.

ONLY THE SHORT SURVIVE

It is true that, when the first atomic bomb was exploded in the deserts of New Mexico, at 5:30 A.M., on July 16, 1945—on the *same* range as that from which the vertiginous disks were seen in 1949—Mars may have observed the flash in so small a part of the Earth. Its redness probably denotes a very far advanced state of cosmic evolution, but we *know* nothing about what sentient or intelligent life may exist in Mars. It may be recalled that dense billowing clouds, seen on the surface of Mars, on January 6, 1950, and, again, on six days on April 1-6, 1950, by an astronomer at Osaka, Japan, were said by him to be gasses of an explosion covering an area of some 700 miles in diameter. He thought they might be volcanic in origin. Mars has a volume one-seventh that of the earth; but we have no proof that the red planet is populated by men of midget, or, indeed, *any* size such as might have been able to stand the terrific pulls of twenty times the Earth's gravitational pull, which were involved in the amazing acceleration of the disks, or white balls seen chasing the rocket over New Mexico.

If they *were* midget-sized beings, who have devised spaceships driven by atomic energy, they would need shields to protect themselves from the lethal and extremely powerful radioactivity which would be radiated and be absorbed by any water or fluid they might carry. And the problem of devising tube, used in these radiation motors, which would not disintegrate under the terrific blasting forth of energy of atomic fission and chain reactions, is not one that we, here, in our atomic experimental stations, appear as yet to have solved. They would also need some means of averting collisions with meteors out in space!

FURTHER SPECULATION ON MIDGET-SIZED ALIENS

It looks as if some of these fantastic theories about midget men from Mars, or some other world, controlling these disks, spheres, or spaceships are based, by analogy, on the relative volumes of the planets compared with that of the Earth, and, therefore, on these theories, may have beings about one-fifth the average stature of terrestrial human beings, say five or six inches. That is, a Martian has a height of about 14 inches, on this theory! This *may* be; but we do not yet know.

If a species of small-sized beings—of course, mere size has little relation to brain power of intellect—are actually manning *some* of these saucers, they may have come from some other planet in the solar system, which has not been detected by our most powerful telescopes. They might even come from the moon, which may not be the entirely airless, waterless waste that is generally supposed! Those who fancy such an unproved theory—and, after all, life seems to be more a matter of air and water, than gravitational pressures—might point to the mysterious lights and vast shadows seen in dark regions of the moon, and usually in the same quadrant of craters, in the 18th century and many times in the 19th century.

IS THERE A FAILURE TO COMMUNICATE?

One risks the charge that one is a *fantaisiste* when one asks if there are attempts of other planets, unknown, to communicate with the Earth; but since the communications cannot possibly be understood, by Earth-people, whether they may be, in fact, trying to send messages to entities who are thought by them to have effected landings on the Earth?

Who can say?

But consider the singular facts that follow:

From time to time, strange words in unknown tongues, or messages come through the ether and are received on radio instruments. In the early days of wireless telegraphy, the late Senator Marconi believed that he received, in the course of wireless experiments at Newfoundland, words in some unknown tongue, which, he theorized, might be from Mars. Anyway, whatever these sounds may have been, they had penetrated the Heavisid-Kenealy layer in the stratosphere, but for whose presence, long wave radio would be impossible, since the electro-magnetic impulses would shoot out into space and not be reflected back towards the Earth. Now, according to *El Diario de Nueva York* (a Spanish newspaper published in New York), on January 31, 1950, something peculiar happened in the midnight skies over Madrid, Spain:

"In the last two days, near midnight, intense phosphorescence and the forms of strange lights have been observed at the same time. They have passed through the sky from north to south, and radio receivers have heard, during the occurrence of this phenomenon, words pronounced in an incomprehensible tongue. Popular fancy supposes that these luminous signals may come from the planet Mars."

THE CRYPTIC FAREWELL OF A VANISHED PLANE

When one is faced with a mystery, it is useful to look round and see if something similar has happened before. Perhaps it has.

On August 2, 1947, the British South American Airways plane, *Lancastrian Star Dust*, mysteriously vanished on a flight over the Andes. She was due to land at the airport at Santiago, Chile, at 5:45 P.M. At 5:41 P.M., she sent out a signal stating her time of arrival. But at the end of the message came the word "Stendec," loud and clear and given out very fast.

The Chilean Air Force operator, at Santiago, queried the word, which he did not understand. He heard it twice repeated by the plane. No explanation of this word has ever been found. Nothing further was heard from the plane, although calls were sent out. The plane never arrived, and, from that day to this, the mystery has never been solved. Searches by ski troops and planes were started, and skilled mountaineers and motor cars hunted all over an area of 250 square miles; but in vain. *Star Dust* carried a crew of five men, and there were six passengers. The pilot, Captain R.J. Cook, had crossed the Andes eight times as second pilot, but this was his first flight as captain. He had been warned at Buenos Aires, and also from London, to take a different route, if bad weather were experienced over the Andes. On the afternoon when this plane vanished, as it seems, in the period of four minutes, a gale of 45 knots was blowing over the Andes, and the El Cristo pass over which he flew was veiled in snow and cloud.

At 5 P.M., 41 minutes before the last message sent was received, Cook radioed the Santiago airport stating he was climbing to 24,000 feet. There is no evidence that his plane overshot Santiago, and fell into the Pacific. Indeed, as, by that time, the plane would have passed from the bad weather zone on the Andes, that possibility seems unlikely.

Aboard the *Star Dust* airliner, when it mysteriously vanished, was a British King's Messenger on a journey for the British Foreign Office. He had spent a hectic career in World War Two, and had spent some time in South America. Ex-police Superintendent Askew, who was senior security officer at the Foreign Office, and among whose staff was the messenger, says: "There were whispers of sabotage, but nothing was ever found to explain the mystery of the airliner *Star Dust* which vanished over South America."

Sabotage has become an overworked explanation. It does *not* explain this cryptic radio signal: "Stendec!"

Who twice sent out that mysterious word "Stendec," which the Chilian operator said was so loud and clear and fast? It came right at the end of the message announcing arrival time, which, as one sees, was four minutes later. Did "something" intercept the plane? If so, what was it?

UFOs Attack Earth . . . The Out of Control Universe of Harold T. Wilkins

Flying Saucers Of Ancient Days

Predating the much better known works of Erich Van Daniken by well over a decade, Harold T. Wilkins discusses the idea that UFOs are not simply a twentieth century phenomenon but instead have their beginnings in very ancient times. Wilkins begins by waxing philosophical about mankind's place in the universe and presents an early version of what has now become a cliché of Ufology, that it would be arrogant of us to presume to be the only life in the universe. He also talks about the things necessary for life on Mars—namely air and water—many years in advance of our own discovery of water on the Red Planet in more recent times. Again, he seems nearly prescient about ideas and facts we now take for granted. Along the way, he recounts the story of a race of homosexual giants who suffered a rain of fire from the sky in the midst of their bizarre coupling, and the appearance in old Ireland of something they called "demon ships."

Behind the singular phenomenon, crudely called the "flying saucers," stands a still unresolved problem: Is Earth the only planet in the solar system that is inhabited by sentient beings?

The thoughts of the ordinary man and woman, if not those of the astrophysicist and the professional astronomer, at once go out to the old red star, the planet Mars, who redness probably indicates an age in evolution much ahead of that of the Earth.

There are curious passages in old English chronicles, written in Medieval Latin, and in Latin incunabula, or books printed before the year 1500 A.D., which suggest that *our Earth may have been under observation by extra-terrestrial visitants for some 1250 years past.* And reports and records as well as astronomical ephemeredes of the days of the old astronomers and mathematicians, such as Herschel, Kepler and Edmund Halley, and reports made to learned journals of the 17th and 18th centuries, by scientists of those days, living in the British Isles, or France, Germany, or Holland and Italy, may also purport *that other planets than Mars* may, also, long ago have *solved the problem of interplanetary travel.*

At the moment, we cannot prove or disprove such theories, or assert that cosmic visitors from planets belonging to systems outside that of our own sun and far away in space have, or have not, visited our own planet. Short of an actual interplanetary trip made from this Earth, or an actual terrestrial landing on the moon, it is not easy to see how such a tremendous riddle can be solved.

The other possible solution would be contact with, or capture of a machine with extraterrestrial visitants aboard, which has ventured into our own atmosphere. Such a possibility seems very unlikely, having regard to differential gravitational forces, and the elusiveness of flying saucers.

Stories of entities from other planets landing in American and Western Europe, in the years 1949 to 1952, are still in the category of "believe it or not." One, at least, is an admitted hoax.

Those who believed that President Truman and the chiefs of the U.S. Navy and War and Defense departments were merely concealing the truth—the author of this book believes they spoke the truth—when they emphatically disowned any connection of the flying saucers with secret experimental devices for offensive or defensive war, may care to glance at the curious historical data, set out below in this chapter. These data considerably broaden the perspective and take it right out of the light of our own day into the far past. It will be seen, indeed, that these weird phenomena range far down the vistas of time into the illimitable past of our Earth. They raise the question again: *Is* there life on planets, or on planets outside our solar system; for after all, is not our system but one of millions of others in an illimitable universe, literally worlds without end?

REQUIREMENTS FOR LIFE ELSEWHERE

In the last resort, the riddle may be reduced not so much to a question of pressures and relative gravitational forces as to the existence of air or water. It is difficult, or impossible, to see how beings with the brain and intellect of men, if not the form of human beings, as we know them in our own planet, could exist without these two essentials for chemico-physical and biotic existence. A priori, it would seem that, unless the accident of life on one cooling star—that of our own Earth—is unique, and has never been and never will be repeated in the comparatively infinite universe, it may not be unreasonable to suppose that, where are and water exist, or where water can be synthesized, and the conditions are not too hot, or too cold, life and intelligence may have arisen on, say, Mars or Venus. The fashionable theory is that our own solar system originated in the million to one cosmic chance of a collision of our proto-sun with some other vast wandering star, torn from its cosmic moorings, or orbital path in space. Either that, or its grazing with the gaseous, incandescent, chemi-metallic envelope of our sun, caused a titanic splitting and centrifugal dispersion, resulting in a sort of vast Catherine Wheel expansion, that threw off the planets circling our sun and born of its gaseous body.

THE HOMOSEXUAL GIANTS

May be, there *is* life on some other planet, for, how otherwise shall we explain what may not necessarily be total legend and myth in the strange stories of South American prehistory, about fire falling from the sky, seemingly by design and not accident, and not as the incalculable explosions of great meteorites, aerolies, comets, or planetoids, upon ancient South American cities?

There is the very ancient Peruvian tradition, of giants who landed near what is now Puerto Viejo. "From the knee down they were as tall as a tall man." Inland, they built great stone houses, and sank splendid stone-lined wells that yielded pure, ice-cold water thousands of years later, in the days of Spanish conquest, in A.D. 1545. One day, when they were engaged in unnatural amours—for they had no women with them, and the native women of old Peru were too small for their lusts—fire from the skies suddenly fell on them in the marketplace. Was this falling of fire merely the cosmic accident of the fall of great aerolites, fireballs, or meteorites, which the naïve myths have garbled, or was it from a spaceship which had hove in sight?

THE VIEW FROM ABOVE

Perhaps, what is more to the point is the remarkable discovery made in 1941, and investigated up to 1946. It was made in the dunes and sandy deserts along the Rio Grande in South Peru. Here, in an area of forty-two miles long and nine miles wide have been found what looks like a vast airdrome, astronomical observatory and center of some solar or planetary cultus combined. On the desert floor are dead straight lines ranging for many miles in parallels, made by removing the pebbles and piling them up in ridges. Some of them seem to be solstitial lines, and there are remarkable figures of a bird, 400 feet long, a spider, or it might be an octopus, for it has eight arms, plants, serpents, animal heads, spirals and geometrical figures. They are thousands of years old. Close by runs the Pan Pacific Highway, and it was the intention of the Government of Peru to build irrigation works which would wholly or partially obliterate these very ancient remains. The place is called the *mesa de Nasca.*

There are remains of ancient stone buildings that may have been observatories, and there are long processional roads and avenues. It has been theorized that these amazing monuments may be associated with lunar and solar cults, or with the periodicity of Venus, Jupiter, Mercury and the Pliades.

But one enigmatic glyph is particularly striking. It is half a mile long, points about due geographical north, and resembles a long, straight rod round which are wound spirals, whose amplitude rises to a peak and then symmetrically decreases, much like a graph on a clockwork or electrical recording instrument. It ends in a series of concentric circles of the whorled type, very like the winder on a fisherman's rod. One suggestive feature characterizes the roads, lines and glyphs in this vast enclosure: they are or were *visible only from the air*, and, indeed, are not visible in all lights. They were found by a pilot of a plane passing over the mesa in a run to the north. They raise a startling and sensational query: were they not merely signals to the planets or the sun, but *indications to an interplanetary spaceship where to land?*

THE COMING OF THE DEMON SHIPS

The old Irish manuscripts have some very singular and quite unexplained reference to "ships seen in the air" and called "demon ships."

The *Speculum Regali in Konungs-Skuggsja*, and also the *Reliquae Antiquae*, tell queer stories of the visit of "demon ships" over the skies of old Ireland. In the *Speculum Regali*, the story, related to the dim and shadowy past of old Eire's heroes and fighting kings, is as follows:

"There happened in the borough of Cloera, one Sunday, while the people were at Mass, a marvel. In this town is a church to the memory of St. Kinarus. It befell than an anchor was dropped from the sky, with a rope attached to it, and one of the flukes caught in the arch above the church door. The people rushed out of the church and saw in the sky a ship with men onboard, floating before the anchor-cable, and they saw a man leap overboard and jump down to the anchor, as if to release it. He looked as if he were swimming in water. The folk rushed up and tried to seize him; but the bishop forbade the people to hold the man, for it might kill him, he said. The man was freed, and hurried up to the ship, where the crew cut the rope and the ship sailed away out of sight. But the anchor is in the church, and has been ever since, as a testimony."

This "demon ship" is also mentioned by Nennius, an Irish chronologist, who lived around 212 or 213 A.D. He says it happened when a man named Congolash was at the fair of Teltown in County Meath.

This version is told in the Irish *Mirabalia*, which means Wonders, cited by the well-known Celtic scholar, the late Kuno Meyer. From the "ship, sailing in the air," one of the crew "cast down a dart at a salmon; but the dart fell down in the presence of the gathering and a man came out of the ship to seize the end of the dart from above, which a man on the ground caught from below. The man above said, 'I am being drowned!' 'Let him go,' said Congolash, and he is let go up and goes from them swimming."

In the *Book of Leinster*, there are said to have been *three ships in the air*, seen from the fair at Teltown, when King Domnall mac Murchada was at the fair. This would be around A.D. 763. In the *Annals*, one reads: "Ships in the air are seen."

THE FEARSOME POWERS OF THE ROWING WHEEL

Another variant of the Irish legend of sky ships—and the old Irish are the nearest to the root stock of the Celts—is that of the "Roth Ramrach," or "Rowing Wheel." It is said to have 1,000 "beds" and 1,000 men in each "bed," and it made sail over land and sea, till it was wrecked by the magic pillar stone of Cnamchoill, an ancient wood near Tipperary. The "Rowing Wheel" is said to have been made by Simon Magus. Simon Magus was the magician who had the misfortune be double-crossed by Saint Peter, in a contest of levitatory flight in the air through a window, and he made the "wheel" with the help of two Irish students of Druidism, Mogh Ruith, the archduke of Erinn, and Ruith's daughter. The "wheel" could sail in the air—and it is certainly strange that some of the strange forms of flying saucers, seen by seaman in the 19th century, in the Arabian Sea, and Indian Ocean, have been in the form of a rolling wheel. The Druid and his daughter, named Tlachtga, carried the remains of the "Rowing Wheel" from the continent of Europe to Ireland. It was in two sections, made of rock, and one piece she set up near Rathcoole, or Raith Chumhaill, County Dublin. These rocks, or pillars, were said to have the power of striking with blindness all who looked at them and with death any who touched them. It was said by the old Irish saint Colum of Cille that the "Rowing Wheel" would pass with destructive power all over Europe, because a "student of every nation was at Simon Magus' school."

Just what is the source of this curious legend—a memory of some sort of spaceship, or saucer of other days—no one can say.

Flying Saucer Humanoids Vs. The Space Monsters

It never ceases to amaze how Harold T. Wilkins had at times a tight grip on what would become the Ufology of the future. In the following story, taken from *Flying Saucers On The Attack*, he again reports on a race of UFO occupants who stand three and a half to four feet tall, the exact same height of the aliens that was to be reported a decade later when the first abduction cases began to be investigated. This is especially relevant when one considers that in the 1950s, when the book was written, UFO occupant cases were nearly non-existent, apart from George Adamski's blonde Venusians, which makes the somber midget workers depicted in Wilkins' work all the more immediate and realistic. This chapter also includes a sighting by a scoutmaster, who was later found wandering in the forest in what has become a frequent feature of alien abduction encounters. And last but not least, there is the stinking horror of Flatwood Hill, West Virginia and the shocked witnesses struggling to cope in its aftermath.

LAYING EYES ON AN ALIEN RACE

We now come to sensational reports of eyewitnesses who say they have seen saucers landing, but who do *not* allege that they have had any communication, whether by word of mouth, or by telepathy or gesture, or any other method. The earliest report is of an event happening on the night of July 2, 1950, and I cite this remarkable and circumstantial story from factory and house magazine, ***The Steep Rock Echo***, of September, 1950, and by permission of the Editor, Mr. B.J. Eyton. It is an organ published by the Steep Rock Iron Company, Ontario, Canada. Mr. Eyton says: "I have been unable either to verify or disprove this story, but about the time it was told and published in our magazine, men working in the mines here at Steep Rock saw a flying saucer at night, and people in the nearby township of Atitokan told the local press that they had seen them in a region between Fort William and Port Arthur, a range of some 140 miles. In fact, one night the telegraphers of the Canadian National Railroads wired to each other to look out for a strange object in the skies, until it reached here. Then it turned back. Everybody is sure he saw a flying saucer that night."

Here is the story published in *The Steep Rock Echo*, September-October 1950:

"In the dusk of July 2, 1950, I and my wife had drawn up our boat on the sandy beach of a tiny cove in Sawbill Bay, where we had gone fishing. Cliffs rise on all three sides of the cove. Small trees and bushes concealed us and our boat from the sight of anyone overhead, in a plane, had there been one around that evening. We had snacks and a thermos flask of tea, and, as the dusk was drawing on, we talked of going home. Suddenly, the air seemed to vibrate as if from shock waves from a blasting operation at the local iron mines. I recollected, however, that the mines were too far away for that. I had an intuition to climb ten feet up a rock, where was a cleft that gave onto the bay.

"I was amazed at what I saw. As I peered through the cleft, taking care to make no noise, I could see out on the bay a large shining object, resting on the water. It was in the curve of the shoreline, about a quarter of a mile away, across the top end of some narrows. I got down from the cleft and sped back to my wife. She was startled as I came running up. 'Why, what on earth is the matter?' she asked. 'Come and see if you see what I see,' I said, grasping her by the arm. 'And make no noise or show yourself.' I drew her by the hand to the cleft. We both peered through it.

"The shining thing was still resting on the water. It looked like two saucers, one upside down on the top of the other. Round the edge were holes like black ports, spaced about four feet apart. We could not see the underside, because the bottom of the thing was resting on the water, or close to it. On top were what looked like open hatches, and moving around over its surface were ten little figures. They looked queer, very queer. Rotating slowly from a central position, and about eight feet up in the air, was a hoop-shaped object. As it rotated, to a point directly opposite to where my wife and I were peering through the rock cleft, it stopped, and the little figures also stopped moving. Everything now seemed concentrated on the little opening through which we were peering. We were about to duck down, as we thought these midget figures might see us and take alarm, when, on the opposite side of the cove, a deer appeared, came to the edge of the water, and stood motionless.

UFOs Attack Earth . . . The Out of Control Universe of Harold T. Wilkins

"We again peered through the cleft in the rock. The little figures and the previously rotating circle were aligned on the deer. But now the circle moved to the left. We ducked down, counted twenty, and took another peep. The thing was gyrating and the figures moving; but the deer didn't seem to trouble them. We ducked down, supposing that a ray had been projected towards the rock from the thing on the water. Maybe the rock was a barrier and kept it off us.

THE FACELESS WORKERS

"It looked as if the whole machine were worked from a central point below the circling ray. The operator was a midget figure on a small raised stand. He wore what seemed to be a red skullcap, or perhaps it was red paint. The caps worn by others were blue. I should say the figures were from 3 feet 6 inches to 4 feet tall, and all were the same size. We could not see their faces. In fact, the faces seemed just blank surfaces! It was odd that the figures moved like automata, rather than living beings.

"Over their chests was a gleaming metallic substance, but the legs and arms were covered by something darker. These figures did not turn around. They just altered the direction of their feet. They walked on the angle, or camber, of the surface of the disk, and the leg on the higher side seemed shorter; so that the compensation—real or apparent—provided against any limp. As I looked, one of the midgets picked up the end, or nozzle, of a vivid green hose. He lifted it, while facing one way, and started to walk the other way. And now the air hummed in a high-pitched note, or vibration. Maybe water was being drawn in, or something was ejected. I do not know if something was being extracted from the water of Sawbill Bay.

"Next time we peered through the rock cleft, we found that all the figures had vanished, and the machine was about eight feet up in the air. I noticed that the water of the lake, near where the thing had rested, was tinged with color combined of red-blue-gold. The disk I reckoned was about 15 feet thick at the center, and some 12 feet at the edges. It tilted at an angle near 45 degrees. Now, there came a rush of wind, a flash of red-blue-gold and it was gone, heading northwards, and so fast that my eye could not follow it. It was now quite dark. We decided to call it a day, and got into our boat and went out into the bay where the saucer had rested on the water. I had aligned two trees to estimate its size, which, I think, was 48 feet. I went back there again, on another day, and as we came through the narrows, I heard a rush of wind, and again something flashed above and beyond the trees. What it was, I could not see. My wife was scared. She said she would never go there again.

THE DISK RETURNS

"A day or two later, I spoke to a friend at the mine, and told him what I had seen. He suggested we both go to the cove on a fishing trip. We had cameras, but after we stationed ourselves at the rock cleft for three evenings running, nothing happened; and on the last evening, we moved quickly along the shore. We patrolled the bay for three weeks, when, one evening, as we were in our outboard motorboat, and a strong wind was cutting across Sawbill Bay, chopping the water, *we saw the disk*! It was in the same spot. I surmise that, as the wind was up from them, they could not hear our motor chugging. I swung her around into the wind, and my friend got the cameras out. But it is difficult to hold a motorboat into the wind on choppy water, while trying to take a photo. Indeed, the wind was so darned cold that my fingers went numb, and I could not manage both the helm and a camera. The boat seesawed up and down so much that my friend could not focus the camera. 'And now,' said he, 'I've seen what you saw, and see!'

"But before we got close up to the saucer, I saw the little figures vanish into the hatches. They had seen us! The rotating mechanism vanished, and the hose reeled in like a flash of green lightning—so fast did they work! There came a regular blast of air and the saucer whizzed off like greased lightning. But my eye was quick enough to see that a little figure, close to the water's edge, was only halfway back to the hatch. He must have operated the end of the green hose, or suction pipe. Our own engine stalled and then ran hot; so we got home late, and our wives were terrified. We had to promise never to go saucer-spotting again!"

THE SCOUTMASTER'S ENCOUNTER

Here follows a story of possibly startled entities on a flying saucer who fired a light-projectile, or put a harmful ray on an intruder:

UFOs Attack Earth... The Out of Control Universe of Harold T. Wilkins

On the night of August 19, 1952, a scoutmaster, D.S. Desvergers, of West Palm Beach, Florida, got out of a car to investigate a strange light in a glade of woods in the Florida Everglades. He came on a thing like half a rubber ball, three feet thick, and high in the center, so that three men could stand erect inside. (Note by Harold T. Wilkins: Other accounts say the object was 30 feet wide, and tapered to three feet on the rims, and that eight men could have been housed in it.) Around the object was a phosphorescent glare. He was seen, and the entities fired at him a ball of that floated slowly at his face. (H.T.W. notes, Another account says that the ball was like a Roman candle.) It singed his hair and face, and burned holes in his cap. Desvergers say he "was blasted"— whether by fear or fright. U.S. Intelligence officers questioned Desvergers, but nothing further has been said. (Summarized from the *Los Angeles Examiner* and New York and Chicago newspapers, some of which add that police found Desvergers wandering in the woods, overcome, and complaining that a dreadful stench accompanied the ball of fire. H.T.W.) Deputy Sheriff Partin found later that the grass in the glade was scorched.

RAISING A STINK

A dreadful stench was also the remarkable feature of the next adventure, which occurred in the dusk of a September night, in 1952. The location was the lonely region of Flatwood Hill, West Virginia, a country of scattered farms and thickly wooded hills.

Half an hour after sunset, on Friday, September 12, 1952, two boys, Eddie May, 13, and Fred May, 12, excitedly told their mother they had seen a saucer land on the top of nearby Flatwood Hill. Mrs. Kathleen May, the mother, her five small sons, and a young National Guardsman, set off for the hilltop, and in the dusk of the starry evening, saw, near a tree, a thing like a half-man, half-dragon, 10 feet tall, with red-orange face and green body. It seemed to glide over the grass towards them, the body all aglow. The whole party fled in terror, increased by an overpowering stench from the visitant. Back in the village, they "vomited for hours." On the same evening, there had been reports of lights and mysterious objects in the skies in that region, and local people said they had seen a silvery disk, jetting a red exhaust, rush at high speed, slow down, and then land on the hilltop. The object that landed had a high-pitched whine and pulsated, and the horrible stench may have been some powerful and irritant gas that it emitted and which encircled the landing place. The saucer is said to have been a large sphere, and some say the noise of a working mechanism came from it.

AN AFTERMATH OF SHOCK

It is surmised that the "dragon-like" entity was wearing a spacesuit and had landed and was returning to the sphere. Mrs. May later said that it was "lit inside and had what seemed to be large and terrible claws." A local editor who went to the hilltop, with five other men, all with shotguns, came onto the hilltop an hour later and saw that something had landed there, left a depression in the soil, and had thrust aside bushes and stones. These men fairly reeled backward from the stench! There were also skid-like marks between the tree where the "monster" had stood and the site of the disk. All the May party had to be treated for shock. The "monster" has been sketched, and appears to have been a very large truncated cone, resting on a smaller cone, with a round, transparent window in front. It projected two small but piercing blue beams. It was the smaller cone that, apparently, looked like half-man, half-dragon. Maybe the "monster" went back to the disk; for it was not seen again. It is also said that, after the incident, "a strange white substance" was picked up where the disk had rested, and sent to for analysis to a laboratory at Charleston, South Carolina. If so, nothing has been revealed, nor has the U.S. Air Force said anything about its investigation of the Flatwood Hill incident.

The local police, however, admit that, on the day of the incident, a fleet of pear-shaped objects, dull red, white, and gleaming had been seen flying in formation over the region, and had hovered in midair, ascended vertically, descended, then flew level, and that three of the strange objects had crashed in the dense woods. Yet the U.S. Air Force authorities declined to explore the woods! It is also said that the disk on the hilltop had been seen to flash a red light which pulsated in a pungent mist.

UFOs Attack Earth . . . The Out of Control Universe of Harold T. Wilkins

UFOs Attack Earth... The Out of Control Universe of Harold T. Wilkins

The Woman From Behind The Moon

It is sometimes said that the 1950s were the Golden Age of flying saucers, and these stories from Harold T. Wilkins' *Flying Saucers On The Attack* definitely add to the plausibility of that statement. Featured here are stories both strange and beautiful, of a contactee who meets an alien woman from the planet Clarion who speaks in rhyme, of a young man hunting in the hills who sees a beautiful woman disembark from a silver ship, as well as brief but crucial mentions of phenomena that would later be a deeply entrenched part of UFO lore, like captured aliens, crashed disks, and autopsies performed on deceased saucer pilots. There is a final round of anecdotes, some of them taken from Rotary Club luncheons, that demonstrate how widespread belief in the UFOs was at the time, when even pillars of the community would speak their minds unashamed.

⚜ ⚜ ⚜

Has anyone ever got inside a flying saucer?

If Mr. Truman Bethurum, a mechanic of California, engaged in road construction work, is to be believed, he is a man who has achieved that success one night, just before dawn, in July, 1953. But exactly as in the case of another gentleman, Mr. George Adamski, of Palomar, California, he has overlooked one trifling "fourth dimensional" obstacle. Both men say they have met entities in saucers who have the power of metamorphosing themselves from our own three dimensional plane of visibility to a fourth dimensional plane wherein they are normally invisible, being entities of a planet of some etheric order of matter whose wavelengths are of a dense matter of the order of invisibility. That is, of matter now our own. Both men see no contradiction in asking these entities to convey them—men of our order of visible matter—to a world which is etheric and invisible, and inhabited by beings who are invisible—to us!

But how, apart from corporeal dissolution, does either of these men suppose that this wonder of a visit by invisible saucer to a fourth dimensional world in space can be achieved *for him*?

A STRANGE AWAKENING

I, as before, summarize this story from various Western American newspapers and journals:

On the time and date stated, Mr. Bethurum, asleep inside a truck parked on State Highway No. 91, some 70 miles west of Las Vegas, Nevada, alleges that he was awakened by people talking outside. The stars were still in the predawn sky, when Bethurum arose from his uneasy seat in the cab and called out: "What's goin' on here?" Outside, he saw eight little men grouped spookily in a semicircle. Mr. Bethurum suspected that there must be a saucer parked nearby. "What about my going aboard her?" he asked the little men. He does not say how they understood him; but he says they took him to the saucer. It will be noted that he was not struck by any paralysis ray, as Mr. Adamski says *he* was, when incautiously approaching *his* saucer from Venus. Mr. Bethurum was led down a corridor past several closed cabin doors, right into a room fitted up like an office and lounge. A very pretty lady confronted him. She was some inches shorter than the men, and had a "Latin appearance." She told him she was captain of the saucer, and a long and highly confidential talk followed. It appears that the little lady was not at all anxious to inform Mr. Bethurum about herself, the crew, or what the saucer was doing in Nevada.

THE SCOW FROM CLARION

One rather odd thing was mentioned by Mr. Bethurum: That the lady spoke English in rhymed couplets!

She said the disk, called a *scow*, came from a planet behind the moon, named *Clarion*, where all is mental and spiritual progress, and an Arcady without war or strife. The crew, who spoke an unknown tongue, were in gray-blue uniform, but only a few came ashore on the Earth at a time. Mr. Bethurum saw no one else in the saucer. The lady-skipper wore a black skirt and red blouse, was four and one-half feet tall, and was a grandmother with two grandchildren, *not* onboard the saucer.

However, Mr. Bethurum did not leave the saucer quite scatheless. He told someone that he brushed against the exterior of the saucer—convex, and like a silver dollar—and at the laundry, later, it was found that large holes, as if caused by acid, had been eaten in his coat and trousers. The lady said they had many flying saucers, all skippered by women, and a crew of 32 men in each. This seems to imply that *Clarion* is a matriarchal planet.

The *scow* had no power motor, but flew in an up-and-down motion, or in steps, along lines of magnetic force. Said the lady to Mr. Bethurum: "I may take five people from Earth to *Clarion*."

Mr. Bethurum told the newspapers that he had eleven meetings with the saucer from *Clarion*. He had another meeting:

Mr. Bethurum and his foreman boss were eating hot dogs and drinking hotter coffee, in a desert café in Nevada, one evening, when, all of a sudden, there entered a mysterious woman, in dark glasses, accompanied by eight little men. A flustered waitress took their orders for, she thinks, cakes and lemonade, and came across to whisper to Mr. Bethurum. Whereupon he went across to the visitants' table and said: "Ma'am, have we met before? Say, ain't these little guys from *Clarion*?" At this very moment, Mr. Bethurum's boss went outside, he said, to keep an eye on where the visitants might go. Whether or not the *Clarion* lady, seeing the sudden exit, suspected that the boss might be looking for a police highway patrol, they all got up and, in military precision, walked to the exit and vanished *into nothingness*!

And that was that!

He has not seen the *Clarion scow* since, but hopes for another encounter. "The U.S. War Department men have been to see me about it, but mum's the word all round," he adds.

ASSORTED SHORTER STORIES

No doubt about it; for another Californian gentleman who alleged that, in 1952, he spoke to a golden-haired five-foot-six man from Venus, by telepathy and gesture, timed from a quarter of a mile away by stopwatch, naively complains that, when *he*, later, invited two official gentlemen from U.S. Governmental intelligence departments to come and see him and his Venusian planetary exhibits, those bored gentlemen listened intently, but registered no surprise on their poker and blasé faces.

UFOs Attack Earth... The Out of Control Universe of Harold T. Wilkins

A young gentleman from Virginia tells me that these stories of encounters with saucers are running all through California like a prairie fire. In England, people are asking why none of these startling things happen *there*?

To them, I suggest attention to the news story following: "Police and firemen returned to Llanberis reporting that their searches for a mysterious object, seen on the slopes of Snowdon, on July 31, 1953, have been fruitless. Police say no aircraft is reported missing." (London newspaper reports, August 2, 1953.)

What, on Snowdon, might attract flying saucers?

In February, 1939, a research engineer reported that he was overcome with a sudden vertigo, while he was prospecting on the slopes of Snowdon, N. Wales. He thought the cause was radioactivity, and he sent samples of the rock which he believed induced the vertigo, to a certain chemical company's laboratory. There may be uranium deposits on Snowdon, but I know that the results of the analysis were never revealed.

THE PURTY WOMAN FROM SPACE

Perhaps less evidential are the stories following: A woman in an Oklahoma township says that, "many years ago," she was traveling in a Conestoga wagon, and on a roadside in Missouri, listened—she was then aged three—to a talk between her father and an old roamer who hove in sight, when the coffee and the hardtack were ready for breakfast in the woods.

"He was an old man, and he told my dad, about 40 years ago (maybe in the 1880s, H.T.W.) he, the old man, was a lad and had gone hunting in the hills, where he saw a round thing settle down from the sky on the bald top of a mountain overhead. He was frightened, but that did not stop him from climbing up the mountain to see who it was. 'It stood in the clearing of some woods, and was like a big silver ball.' Soon, a piece of the top slid back and two things came out. Said the old man: 'They wuzzn't as tall as me; but sure was nice-lookin' folks. Hadn't much on their purty bodies and legs, that's sure; but the gal wuz as purty as a filly on a medder in the spring a-foolin' round and raisin' the passions of an old spavined stallion, and then kickin' her heels and dashin' off. They tried to talk to me, but neither of us could understand what the other said. I was too scared to say much. Then they stepped back into the ball, slid back the lid, and the ball went up into the sky till it was lost to my eyes. Yep, it's the doggone truth, I'm tellin' yo', though smarties round this location say I alwuz was loco.'"

EARLY COVER-UP RUMORS

A man in Oregon wrote a letter to a friend of mine in Oklahoma, about what his son, a U.S. Marine on the way to his depot at Fort Pendleton, overheard, in December 1951, at the famous observatory at Palomar, California, the site of the world's largest telescope:

"I and another marine were chatting to one of the Palomar professors when a friend of his arrived from Berkeley, California. He, too, is a professor. They began talking, and we listened in to what we were not supposed to hear. The Palomar man said that the U.S. Federal Bureau of Investigation had forbidden the publication of astrophysical photos taken at Palomar. 'Why?' asked the other. 'Well, they show things which the U.S. Government think it wiser people should not know. They might cause panics. There are pictures of jet planes chasing flying saucers, and disintegrating in midair. There are data about strange changes in the atmosphere, and the effect on other planets of radioactive emanations after the explosion of atomic bombs. I have heard, too, a strange story that a landing field has been found in one of the Australian deserts, whose origin in unknown. The Australian Royal Air Force authorities are said to have cordoned off the area, and no one is allowed in there. They are trying to find the origin of the landing field, which they do not believe was made by any terrestrial being."

I have a friend in Australia, whose son is an officer in the Australian Air Force. He passed my inquiry to his son, who replied: "A spaceship *could* have landed in one of our deserts, for they are just one hell of a place, and there are plenty of blank spaces. If Mr. Wilkins can find out the supposed date of the landing, I should be interested."

I do not know the date. Some time later, in 1952, my friend wrote that he wondered if the alleged unknown landing field were one of those made in World War II—at the time there was a trek from Darwin, in N.W. Australia—when the Japanese bombed it from the air. In June, 1952, I got a reply: "Our Australian Air Authorities, when shown your report about an alleged landing ground of a flying saucer, or spaceship said, 'We have no comment to make.'" So? My reply is: "Then have you something you wish to hide from the public, that is not concerned with security matters?"

Walter Winchell, the well-known columnist stated: "June 30, 1952: Scientists at Palomar Observatory, California, are supposed to have seen a 'spaceship' land in the Mojave Desert, in May last. Four persons stepped out, took one look, and went off again. The U.S. Army may officially announce it in the fall."

Needless to say, the U.S. Army made no such announcement at *any* date!

A CHRISTMAS MORNING ABDUCTION?

Evidently, there are people in the U.S.A. who believe that flying saucer entities have kidnapped human beings! In July, 1953, one George Sodder, of Fayetteville, North Carolina, put up a billboard, on which was the following announcement:

"I offer $5,000 for information about the fate of five children, mysteriously snatched away from a burning house, on Christmas morning, 1945. The parents escaped, but at first they believed the children had perished in the flames, supposed to be caused by faulty wiring. But no remains were found in the ashes. A bus driver says he had seen balls of fire thrown on the roof."

CAPTURED ALIENS

Other reports, confirmable or otherwise, have reached me. They are fairly sensational, but probably would not come with a British High Court's rules of evidence:

"A little man from a saucer is being tenderly cared for in the incubator room at San Diego, while cadavers of two saucer pilots are being dissected by surgeons of the U.S. Army Air Force (Medical Division). A Californian air pilot told me that, in 1942, he had been right inside a giant saucer, and seen giant flywheels sheathed in metal skins, and found that the motive-force came from electrostatic turbines, whose flywheels create an electromagnetic field of force, creating tremendous speeds. The little saucer men have a smaller bony structure than Earth-men, but the bones are proportionally heavier, and their stomachs smaller." (H.T.W., This report comes from Mr. Joe Rohrer of Pikes Peak Radio Company, at a Chamber of Commerce luncheon, in Pueblo, Colorado, on July 22, 1952.)

Letter from a correspondent in Oklahoma, to Harold T. Wilkins, the author of this book (July 24, 1952): "On a business trip to San Francisco, last week, I met a nice reliable fellow who has heard from a pal in the U.S. Air Force, that they have captured a little fellow, three feet tall, from a forced-down saucer, and are keeping him alive in a pressure chamber, somewhere in California. He comes from another planet, and was one of three others killed in a crash caused by radar, in an Arizona desert, in 1950. They are showing him pictures and teaching him to read and write, and understand."

LOOSE TALK FROM AROUND THE COUNTRY

I offer no comment on the following stories: From *The Buffalo Evening News*, August 27, 1952: "A man at Lamberton N.C., says a thing 8 feet long and 6 feet wide, landed in his yard after knocking bricks off his chimney. A man about 2 feet 6 inches tall came out and stood by the thing. 'I asked him if he was hurt. He scrambled in, and it went away with a whistle and a whiff, and loud noise.'"

"Three saucers are known to have landed, and one of the inmates, stepping out, died on his own doorstep. The space visitors can't get acclimatized to our atmosphere. The U.S. Government are deliberately confusing folks and hiding the truth." (From Mr. S. Farwell, special agent of the General Electric Company, speaking at a Rotary luncheon in Los Angeles, California, on August 29, 1952.)

In March, 1953, Mr. N. Bean, a research engineer, startled listeners at a Rotary Club affair, held at Miami Beach, Florida, by stating: "I have personally talked with a truck driver who hauled a forced-down flying saucer from New Mexico to a place in Ohio. The driver told me that the U.S. authorities have been unable to find a way to open the saucer. But I can't accept as positive that little men have been found in saucers; though on March 31, 1953, I saw a whole squadron of saucers, in formation, over Golden Beach, near Miami, Florida."

UFOs Attack Earth . . . The Out of Control Universe of Harold T. Wilkins

October 8, 1953: "Yesterday, in New York City, a high, thin voice interrupted a radio show which was boosting a book on saucers. It said: 'You Earthmen will soon be annihilated, and your planet, unless you stop talking about flying saucers. I am speaking from a spaceship over Los Angeles, California.' Later, the same voice came on the air, saying, 'I am over Salt Lake City. You cannot see me, but I can reach you easily. If you saw my hideous face, it would scare you to death.' The radio concern and author and publisher deny any knowledge of this affair." (Taken from various New York City newspapers.)

UFOs Attack Earth . . . The Out of Control Universe of Harold T. Wilkins

The Magic Venusians

Harold T. Wilkins was not one to suffer fools gladly. He also had little patience with those he considered to be hoaxers. In the following excerpt, taken from this 1955 book *Flying Saucers Uncensored*, he relates a story about two blue-skinned Venusians who visit a newspaper office seeking publicity because it would "help" them. Claiming to have recently landed in the Mojave Desert, they eventually are hired to work in a Los Angeles municipal office where they show a marked talent for finding missing persons. The excerpt also contains the story of a contactee named simply Orfeo, who converses for two hours with a male and female alien who apparently held strong anticommunist convictions. Wilkins then explains why he feels that the two narratives may spring from the imagination of a California freelance writer, though he wisely leaves the ultimate verdict in the hands of the reader. One is reminded that Budd Hopkins and other UFO researchers believe that aliens may walk among us in essentially human form and that it would be impossible in many instances for us to tell any difference, though the Venusians here at least have their telltale blue skin. Whether the stories are hoaxes or not, they still offer a fascinating look at contactee accounts of the 1950s and Ufology in its naïve youth.

The following was mailed to me, in good faith but not undue credulity, by a well-educated Californian:

"In March, 1953, a Los Angeles journalist had a strange caller at his office, a tall man, dressed in loose and shoddy clothing, whose skin had a curious bluish pigmentation. He told the clerk in the inquiry office: 'I am a man who has recently landed in your state from what you call a flying saucer. We set it down on the floor of the Mojave Desert. I wish to have some publicity in your newspaper, for it would help both me and your Earth.'

"'Oh, yeah!' said the clerk, with a grin which changed to a look of surprise as he took in the queer appearance of the caller. 'Wait a minute, pal, while I ring up the City Editor!'"

Now, newspapers are accustomed to queer-looking and eccentric callers, and on most of them a reporter is assigned the not always enviable job of tactfully getting rid of them. I have had this job in my own time as a London newspaperman, and well know the difficulty of one sometimes has with them. I well remember one man with a wild eye and an unearthly manner who, when I asked him his name and business, presented me with a card on which was the one word "God!" I imagine that it was not always harmless sort of caller that the City Editor had in mind, when the clerk gave his impressions of the blue-skinned caller:

"The City Editor rang up one of his reporters. 'Sounds screwball to me,' he said, 'but perhaps you'd better see him. He may be loco, but you may get a few lines out of him. There's been so much recently about these flying saucers. See what the guy has to say.'

THE QUEER PEAS IN A POD

"The caller told Jim Phelan, the reporter, that he would call back next day with another man who, like himself, came from the planet Venus. Phelan thought that would be the last he would see of this crackpot. However, the queer man called back next morning with another queer being. The two were as much like each other as two peas in a pod. Both were six foot six in height. Their skin has the bluish tinge one often sees in cardiac cases. But it later appeared that heart disease was *not* their trouble. Both were emaciated. The clothes they wore looked as if they had come out of a sailor's slop shop. Very loose in fit and shoddy. When the reporter looked closely at their heads, he was struck by their ears, which were pricked, like those of a breed of Asiatic dogs. Their hands, too, were queer—they seemed to be jointless.   "'Where d'ye say you come from?' asked Phelan.

"'Venus!'

"'Huh, I s'pose you mean the planet of that name? How did you get here?'

"'We landed in our little disc-ship in the Mojave Desert, and walked and what you call hitchhiked here from San Bernadino.'

"'What happened to your saucer? Is it still there in the desert?'

"The Venusians smiled, looked at each other, but did not answer. After a minute, one of them said: 'We find the climate of South California dreadfully hot and sultry, even in winter.'"

This must import that these queer beings did not come from the planet Venus, since that planet's upper layer of cirrus clouds, and it's comparative proximity to the sun, much nearer than the earth, ensures that it receives twice the amount, or even more, of solar heat than does the earth. Whether they came from Venus, as a way station from, or in relation to some other possibly "etheric," or fourth-dimensional double of some visible planetary world (and the up-to-date astronomer now talks of "planetary doubles" H.T.W.), is something on which light may be thrown as the flying saucer drama moves towards its inevitable climax.

The interrogation proceeded:

"'Why do you come to Earth?'

"'We come to study your minds and your thought and your scientific knowledge. That is why we travel through space.'

"'What do you want from this paper?'

"'We want publicity, as that will help us to travel.'

"Phelan explained that a story would get them more than they bargained for; that the publicity might lead to their being both shut up in a lunatic asylum, or put under detention in some camp controlled by the military or security authorities.

"One of them spoke quickly: 'Please do not give us this publicity.'

"Said Phelan: 'How come you speak English so well?'

"'We learnt it listening to your radio and television broadcasts.'"

THE FINGERNAIL OF PROOF

Then, according to my Los Angeles friend's story, a remarkable incident occurred. The reporter challenged them to prove that they came from some world in space.

"One of the 'Venusians' walked over to a desk made of very hard wood. With his fingernail he scored in the hard wood a furrow nearly a quarter of an inch deep!

"'Does that satisfy you?' he asked the reporter. 'If not, I can throw the whole desk out of the window onto the street below.'

"'No, that satisfies me. Say, call back here tomorrow and I'll see if I can find you a job.'

"It appears that Phelan persuaded a pal to give these queer guys a job in a law office of a department run by the municipality of Los Angeles. While there these strange beings were given a piece of steel. In this, one of them made with his thumbnail an indentation more than one-half inch deep! It was found that these strange beings had peculiar powers of another sort. They were put on to trace lost and missing persons, and they traced them in two-and-a-half hours compared with the two to three weeks required by even the best departmental sleuths! Naturally, men who were working in the office, and had not been told about this story of their having come from Venus, were curious about their remarkable powers.

"Someone was so impressed, or so suspicious, that he communicated with the F.B.I., which sent an investigator. But, as if in some strange way, the 'Venusians' had telepathic powers, or some faculty of prevision, they did not turn up at the office. The F.B.I. have never been able to find them for questioning, but I am assured there is a report about this queer affair in the secret F.B.I. files."

The steel, indented more than one-half inch deep, is said to have been sent for analysis to the laboratory of a metallurgical chemist. To have such an effect on steel, the report said, pressure of at least 1,800 pounds to the square inch would have been necessary, and the steel would have been fractured rather than indented! Moreover, what was even more remarkable, in the furrow made in the steel by the 'Venusian' man, were fourteen elements not present in the rest of the steel. (It would be interesting to know if any of these elements are unknown in the Mendeleyev system, elements not yet known, or not actually existing on our own Earth! H.T.W.)

ANOTHER CONTACTEE CONVERSES

What comment is one to make on this story?

This: That one of the men, circulating it in an American magazine, is a highly imaginative freelance writer. In 1953, this gentleman was told, by another Californian gentleman, another story of an alleged landing of saucer entities, which the former wrote up very nicely, not to say transcendentally. From this, it appears that the second gentleman is, or was, a plastic worker in a factory, manufacturing plastic installations for American Air Force radarscopes. Homeward bound, on May 24, 1952, after his nightshift, he became the reluctant hero of a strange adventure. He was driving his car when he saw ahead of him, in the sky, a glowing red object which appeared to be trailing him, and radiating something which gave him a "queer prickling electrical sensation." Suddenly, the strange orb shot up into the sky, hovered, and released two small green, fluorescent discs which came to a rest a few feet above his car. Out of the discs came a voice speaking perfect English:

"Have no fear, Orfeo, for we are friends. You are communing with friends from another planet."

The discs then projected a sort of screen on which appeared the radiant heads of a most noble man and woman, with whom Orfeo had "telepathic talk" lasting for the rather unprecedented space of two hours by the clock. One of these telepathic "communicators" made the astounding statement that every man, woman and child "is recorded in our vital statistics on crystal discs!"

The communicator added, as has been the case in other alleged encounters of saucer entities by California gentlemen, that Orfeo was specially favored, he "being one of three human beings selected for communication." The others live in India and Italy. It is to be noted that this communicator gave Orfeo a singularly inaccurate account of the death of Captain Thomas Mantell, killed in January 1948, when his plane disintegrated over Godman Airfield, near Fort Knox, Kentucky. Mantell had been ordered to close with an unidentified flying object of *vast size*, but the communicator told Orfeo that it was merely a *small disc*. It may be presumed that the prodigious "crystal recording discs" are not *quite* invariably reliable as "vital statisticians."

UFOs Attack Earth ... The Out of Control Universe of Harold T. Wilkins

At the end of this two hours talk *by telepathy* the discs vanished into the blue, after promising to contact Orfeo later. But it was not until 10 P.M., on July 23, 1952, that on a "vacant lot," Orfeo saw a thirty-foot-wide object aground. He entered it, and by telepathic command, sat on a translucent chair. Orfeo was then taken for a ride into the empyrean from which he looked down on a huge globe enhaloed by rainbows. "It is your Earth," he was told telepathically.

Then he saw, out in space, a thing like a vast dirigible, at least a thousand feet long and ninety feet high. From it came the music of the spheres. There were three decks, but no visible occupants. It had "rotors" of flame at each end. He was then returned to Earth in the United States, and commanded telepathically to tell the scoffing earthlings about his adventure. He was then started on a nationwide lecture tour under the spiritual sponsorship of a Buffalo, New York, elder who habitually broadcasts to the sound of trumpets and shawms and quartets of "quiring" ladies and gentlemen who nightly make the welkin ring with loud hosannas.

Orfeo had another encounter with the saucer entity about 2 P.M., on August 2, 1953. This time, a gentleman came out from under the shadows of a road bridge, clad in a seamless blue suit. Orfeo was given a glance at prehistory, and some account of an Elysian world from which man fell when he blasted the planet Lucifer, rotating between Mars and Jupiter.

The entity discoursed on a neo-Oriental, Maya illusion of a world of sin and sorrow, and on communism and left-wingerism with which venomous snakes were compared greatly to the detriment of the reds. Oddly enough, the saucer entity ended this edifying conversation by asking for a drink. Orfeo departed to fetch from the nearest drug store a bottle of pop, hesitating apparently to demoralize "Neptune," as he called his etheric visitor, by treating him to a flagon of the stronger brew that comes from Milwaukee.

A THREE DOLLAR "BILL"?

The Santa Monica, California, gentleman who imparts the atmosphere to this sprightly story, himself tells another about this strange man who rang him from Los Angeles:

"Call me Bill," said the stranger. "I am coming to Santa Monica just to see you."

At 6 P.M., on a day in June 1953, "Bill" appeared "out of the blue," dematerializing, so to speak, close to a bus stop on the Santa Monica Boulevard. According to the imaginative Santa Monica freelance, "Bill" also proved to be a six-foot-sixer, with a strange, whitish-blue skin and complexion, high cheekbones, a sort of Oriental countenance, and psychic qualities, "full of vibrations." One gathers it was "Bill" who put the Santa Monica freelance onto Orfeo, of whose existence the Santa Monican was previously unaware. According to "Bill," Orfeo was the first terrestrial gentleman ever to make a trip to outer space in a flying saucer.

(H.T.W. This claim will be violently and vehemently denied by other Californians, who allege that they anticipated Orfeo's adventure by two to three years. Theirs, they imply, is the only true story, all others being shams, as the Old Newgate Gaol chaplain said of his ballad books and last dying speeches of old English pirates about to be swung off scaffolds.)

"Bill," said they, from outer space, had commissioned him to request he Santa Monica freelance to act as a literary "ghost" to Orfeo, whose own education was not quite equal to the task. "Bill" also put the Santa Monican in touch with a Los Angeles newspaper reporter who rather reluctantly spilled the mystic beans.

However the truth may lie, in regard to the mysterious entity who could, with his bare fingers, cut his name and address, had he so wished, in cold steel, I must leave my reader to form his or her own opinion about the cold objectivity, or the warm and vibrant romance of Orfeo's and the Santa Monica gentleman's narrations. All I wish to say is that another Santa Monican resident writes me that after reading "Bill's" story, he got on the telephone to the other Santa Monican, and made an appointment to meet him. Alas! the freelance failed to turn up as he promised, and has never since communicated with his telephone friend and candid inquirer.

From documents reaching me by the courtesy of American correspondents, it appears that many of these concocters of romantic stories appear to be backing each other up, apparently on the assumption that if they do not hang together they will hang separately. How much pure or impure psychopathy is intermingled with these romantic stories it would be unprofitable to say. But this I *may* say: these far from veracious stories do cover a very serious theme with ridicule, and the derision of scoffers who are thus given an appearance of justification.

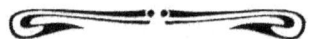

UFOs Attack Earth . . . The Out of Control Universe of Harold T. Wilkins

Tales of Teleportation

Harold T. Wilkins was fascinated by Fortean phenomena, as the following chapter demonstrates, though he often connected that type of anecdote with the flying saucers that "peopled" the skies of the era in which he wrote *Flying Saucers Uncensored*, the early 1950s. In the excerpts quoted here, Wilkins relates several stories of what can best be described as incidents of teleportation, the mysterious movement through space and time from one physical location to another, or from one dimension to another. History is full of stories of the unexplainable appearance of apparent "victims" of teleportation, who suddenly find themselves in a strange world where they do not speak any earthly language, or even, as in one case in this chapter, are totally and completely ignorant of even the most commonplace human customs or practices. This chapter also includes the frightening experience of a couple staying in a hotel in Bristol, England, who are awakened by strange noises and then confronted by an opening in the floor that seems to be trying to drag the husband into its unseen depths, what Wilkins calls a "frustrated" attempt at teleportation. He concludes by arguing that teleportation is but one more aspect of the flying saucers' apparent capabilities.

I shall tell below of a very eerie modern case of apparently frustrated or inhibited teleportation, in the city of Bristol, in the age of railroads. Here are other cases of possible teleportation—only the few permitted by the space at my disposal.

January 5, 1900: Sherman Church, a young fellow employed in the Augusta Mills, at Battle Creek, Michigan, has mysteriously vanished. He was seated in the company's office when he arose and ran into the mill. He has not been seen since. The mill has been taken almost to pieces by searchers, and the river, woods, and country scoured, but to no avail. No one saw Church leave town, nor was there any known reason for his doing so. (*Chicago Tribune*, January 5, 1900.)

UFOs Attack Earth... The Out of Control Universe of Harold T. Wilkins

April 15, 1851: In December, 1850, a mysterious stranger was found wandering in a village near Frankfurt-on-Oder, in Brandenburg, Prussia. No one knows how he got there. He knew very little German. Taken to Frankfurt, he said his name was Joseph Vorin, and that he had come from Laxaria, in Sakria, which is far from Europe, "beyond vast oceans."

August 1869: Thirteen children mysteriously vanished in Cork, Ireland. In the same month Brussels, Belgium, was agitated about the numbers of missing children. In both cases, there was no suggestion of kidnapping—no ransom notes or other signs.

April 23, 1885: Isaac Martin, a young farmer of Salem, Virginia, went into a field to work and disappeared. Other people in this region have mysteriously vanished.

1888: Five "wild men" and a "wild girl," speaking unknown tongues, appeared in Connecticut on January 1.

July and August, 1892: In Montreal, so many people mysteriously vanished that every other day, the newspaper headlined the events with: "Another Missing Man." Similar mysterious disappearances had occurred in the same city in July, 1883.

1895: While detectives were investigating the disappearance of a little girl named Rooney, in Belfast (August 3), a little boy, named Webb, vanished, followed by another child, and by a third. On September tenth and twelfth, two more small boys vanished in Belfast.

1920: Eight small girls, all under twelve, mysteriously vanish in Belfast. The people are in a commotion.

January 10, 1905, and following days: A man who spoke in a language none could understand, and whose manner was "wild" and strange, was arrested by a metropolitan policeman, in a London street. Detectives from Scotland Yard said he carried a book in which he appeared to have made sketches of things he had seen along the roads. In the book were writings of which linguists told Scotland Yard: "We do not know what language they are written in; it is not Turkish, Bohemian, Czech, Russian, Polish, Arabic, Persian or Hebrew."

September 18, 1905: "Le Matin" of Paris reports that a young man, arrested in a Paris street, and charged with vagrancy, speaks a tongue no linguist understands. In vain have Orientalists and experts in European or African tongues spoken to him; but by the language of signs, he has made known that he comes from "Lisbian.' He says the Lisbian word for chair is "eisar"; table, "lotoba," and "sonar" means nose; God was "Odir," house was "sacar."

1906: On October 15, a young woman was arrested in Paris, charged with picking pockets. She answered in an unknown language, which no expert in European or Asiatic tongues understood.

1926: In early November, a whole series of mysterious disappearances of people—eight in three days—in Southend, Essex: a mother and two small children; girls aged fifteen and sixteen.

THE LITTLE GIRL FROM NOWHERE

Another mystery that has a suggestion of teleportation about it: On the evening of April 3, 1817, a strange girl appeared at the door of a cottage near Brislington, Bristol. She spoke an unknown tongue, and signed that she wanted food. Later, a Bristol magistrate, Samuel Worrall, took her to his home at Knowle Park, as she was a very "prepossessing young woman." (H.T.W. Whether Worrall was animated by the same feelings as those of a London archdeacon who, in 1920, attracted the notice of the London police by what *they* regarded as his suspiciously benevolent interest in pretty young women, we will leave the cynics to investigate.) Worrall's protégé wrote in characters said to look like "frying pans, combs, and bird cages." Experts at Oxford University could not identify them. Mrs. Worrall, no doubt with entirely disinterested reasons, shipped the girl out to America, and paid her passage at least *one way*. In Philadelphia, the girl gave public exhibitions of her mysterious writing. Thereafter she dropped out of sight.

THE BOY WHO KNEW NOTHING

Some eleven years later there came through the gate of the old walls of Nuremberg, Germany, a strange boy who appeared unacquainted with the most ordinary objects and experiences of human beings. He snatched with delight at the pretty flame of a burning candle and was scorched. A certain Professor Daumer, who took him to his house, found him very intelligent. The boy soon learnt to speak German, though with a queer accent. Later on, he said he had been shut up in a dark room, and tended by a man who taught him only two German sentences. Eyewitnesses, who saw the boy soon after he entered Nuremberg, said his color was too healthy for him to have been confined for any length of time. On December 14, 1833, five years later, he ran out of a park at Anspach, Bavaria, crying: "I have been stabbed!" and soon died. No weapons were found and no other footprints than his own in the newly fallen snow. The autopsy showed that his heart had been pierced by something that had cut through his diaphragm, penetrating heart and liver. Doctors agreed that the wound could not have been self-inflicted. There are suggestions of amnesia about this strange affair—which *may* point towards teleportation, perhaps from some other world in space!

Herr von Feuerbach, who had interested himself in this mysterious boy from the first, wrote:

"He showed such complete deficiency in words and ideas, such perfect ignorance of the commonest things and appearances of nature, such horror of all customs, conveniences, and necessities of civilized life, and, moreover, such extraordinary peculiarities in his social, mental and physical disposition, that one might feels oneself driven to believe him to be a citizen of another planet, transferred by some miracle to our own."

His name? Kaspar Hauser, one of the greatest enigmas of history.

FLEEING FROM THE UNKNOWN

A final incident.

At four-thirty, on December 9, 1873, the Night Superintendent, T. Harker, of the Bristol and Exeter Railway, at Temple Meads, joint station, was sitting in his office, poking up the coal fire into a blaze. Outside, a nipping wind blew from the northeast. The down express from Derby and the North to Bristol, and the connecting express from Paddington, London, were not due for an hour. The station was all in shadows. The few flickering gas lamps but dimly lit up the dark spaces from the bleak isle of iron pillars. The sort of early morning not fit for a dog to be abroad.

On a sudden, the silence was rent by a scream of "Murder! Murder!"

UFOs Attack Earth ... The Out of Control Universe of Harold T. Wilkins

Down the platform, on bare feet, frantically bounded a woman, disheveled, wildly excited, clad only in a Victorian nightdress. Behind her ran a man, also in nightdress, but with a smoking pistol in his hand. Both kept glancing anxiously behind them.

The woman stopped at the door of Harker's office and beat with her fists upon the panels. Knocking over his office chair, the startled Harker opened the door.

The woman screamed at him: "They will murder us! They have followed us onto this station. I demand that you search the waiting rooms."

Harker shouted and two porters raced up, rubbing the sleep out of their eyes.

"Stay here in my office," he said to the man and woman, "whilst these men and I make a search."

Harker and the porters hunted all around the big bleak station, but found no one.

Returning to his office, he found the man so agitated that he stammered badly, and Harker could not understand a word he said. Concluding that the two were either drunk or mad, Harker sent a porter to fetch a town policeman. The sequel was heard next day in Bristol Police Court, and the **London Times** of December 11, 1873, headed the story:

"Extraordinary Hallucination at Bristol Police Court Yesterday. Thomas B. Cumpston and his wife, Mrs. Annie Martha Cumpston, of Virginia Road, Leeds, Yorkshire, were brought up before the magistrates for being disorderly at the Victoria Hotel, Bristol, and letting off firearms. It is said by the landlady of the hotel, Mrs. Tongue, that the defendants took an apartment at the hotel, on Monday evening. They retired to rest at about 12 o'clock. About 4 A.M., she was awakened by loud screams and shouts in their bedroom, succeeded by reports of firearms. She went down and found that they had both leapt from their bedroom into the yard, twelve feet below. They then both made their way to the railroad station opposite.

"Mr. T. Harker, night superintendent of the Bristol and Exeter Railway, said the Cumpstons rushed into his office partly dressed, and crying out, 'Murder!' They were in a terrible state of excitement. They told me they had escaped from a den of rogues and thieves, and they had had to defend themselves. They were under the impression that someone was following them, and that made me search the waiting room to see that no one was there. Upon my sending for a policeman, Mr. Cumpston was searched and a revolver and three knives were found on him. (H.T.W. It is curious that a respectable English Victorian, in 1873, should arrive in Bristol carrying a revolver and three knives! Had he experienced similar adventures prior to 1873?)

"Asked by the magistrates what they had to say, Cumpston, who has an impediment in his speech, said that he and his wife had been staying at Clifton, two miles away; but, intending to proceed to Weston-super-Mare in the morning, they came to Bristol and engaged a room at the Victoria Hotel, being near the railway station. They were alarmed at about 4 A.M. by terrible noises they could not explain, and were badly frightened. The bed seemed to open, and he heard all sorts of strange things. The floor, too, opened and they heard voices. They were so terrified that they opened their bedroom window and leapt out.

"Mrs. Cumpston gave her version of the affair. She said: 'We heard terrible noises at 4 A.M. The floor seemed to be giving way. It certainly opened. My husband fell down some distance, and I tried to get him up. What we said was repeated every time we spoke!' Being very much frightened, she asked her husband to fire off his pistol, which he did, into the ceiling. The noises continuing, they got out of the window, but she did not know how. When they got outside, she asked her husband to fire off his pistol again. Then they ran up to the railway station.

"She told the Bench that she did not hear the noises so plainly as her husband. Ultimately, a Mr. Butt, telegraphed to come from Gloucester, attended the Court and told the magistrates that the couple occupied a very good position in Leeds. He offered to take proper charge of them if they were handed over to him, which was ultimately done, the defendants being discharged from custody. No explanation can be given of this strange affair, and the belief is that it was the husband's hallucination."

THE TERRIFYING ABYSS

The *Bristol Post* added more details:

"As Cumpston was about to be dragged into the opening in the floor, his wife says she dragged him back. In Court, Cumpston's excitement was still so intense that he could not clearly express himself. Mrs. Cumpston also said that, earlier in the evening, they had both been alarmed by loud sounds, but the landlady reassured them. At three or four in the morning, the sounds were heard again. They jumped out on the floor, which was giving way under them. Voices, repeating their exclamations were heard, or their own voices echoed strangely. Then, according to what she saw, or thought she saw, the floor opened wide. Her husband was falling in to the opening, and she dragged him back. The landlady was called, and she testified that the sounds had been heard, but she was unable to describe them clearly. Policemen said they went to the Victoria Hotel, examined the bedroom, but found nothing to justify the extraordinary behavior of the Cumpstons. They suggested it was a case of collective hallucination."

ARE THE FLYING SAUCERS BEHIND IT ALL?

Of course, it was nothing of the kind! I draw notice here, as in other cases, to the strange noises preceding and accompanying the phenomenon. If the discreet and businesslike landlady did not let her own tongue run about these noises, her reasons would be obvious. It would hardly be a good advertisement for the hotel to let people say it was "haunted."

The very mysterious phenomenon of teleportation is well known to students of the occult and in the annals of psychical research. Those who have experienced it—often young children—show amnesia. They have no recollection, afterwards, of what occurred in the long or short interval when they were mysteriously missing. Teleportation might be defined as the act of opening a vortex in matter and bringing it from one form through another. In some of its very mysterious aspects, it reaches from the chemico-physical world into the unseen.

It is possible that, in this phenomenon, a physical body, either animate or inanimate, is reduced to its "etheric state" by the "condensing form," and the being or object is transported to a point in the vast universe. Some of these aeroforms of the non-terrestrial, fourth dimensional, or, if one prefers, "intra-dimensional" types, appear to have the amazing power of passing themselves and their saucer-discs from one plane to another, including that of our three-dimensional Earth!

UFOs Attack Earth . . . The Out of Control Universe of Harold T. Wilkins

UFOs Attack Earth . . . The Out of Control Universe of Harold T. Wilkins

Monster Of Mystery And A Strange Skeleton

Strange Mysteries of Time and Space is the last book by Harold T. Wilkins that we will be examining pages from, but it is certainly not his least. We begin this chapter with his preface to the 1958 paperback edition, in which he talks of how his travels to the actual sites of many of the mysteries he writes about are an essential part of his writing process, although the attempt to answer some questions often leads only to further questions. Also included here is a story of a monstrous skeleton discovered in Belgium, a tale told to Wilkins when he rented a room in the same former monastery where the gruesome find was first unearthed. Wilkins speculates that the skeleton could be the grim remains of some perverted, unnatural coupling, or even that it was teleported to Earth from another world. Also recounted here is the story of an unsolved murder that took place in Liverpool, England, sometime in the late nineteenth century—the kind of mystery we would call in the Cold Case Squad for in our time. Wilkins chides the police of his time for failing to follow up on some obvious clues, and invokes the name of Sherlock Holmes in all his sarcasm.

PREFACE

After half a century of travels by train, ship and air, or on shank's mare, into out-of-the-way parts of the world, the author has found that it is essential, where possible, to visit in person the location of a mystery. And he has been forced to recognize that, in trying to solve *one* mystery, he has often unearthed another mystery which, at first seeming to hold the clue to the first, yet, in the end, may prove either to be a false trail or merely to heighten the *first* mystery that he has been investigating. It is a truism—but one by no means generally recognized—that there is nothing stranger than the mind of man. When men and women lose the sense of mystery, life will prove to be a gray and dreary business, only with difficulty to be endured. But that *any* fool can entertain was, alas, a silly saying of the late Bernard Shaw! If the reader finds entertainment in this book, the author will have achieved his main purpose.

THE MONSTER OF BRUGES

Our twentieth century—the age of two devastating world wars; of relativity; the coming of interplanetary travel, still, however, a long way off in the future; the diabolical hydrogen bomb and the fearful weapons of intercontinental ballistic missiles; and of the years ahead of which no man cares to take a long view—has certainly seen no lack of mysteries as baffling as any that were in the centuries before.

Some years before the Second World War, I was in that city of slow time and the sound of dreamy carillons, where, if there are not now "grass-grown streets trodden by noiseless feet," there is certainly a strange labyrinth of twisting medieval streets in which it is easy for a stranger to get lost all night. I refer to Bruges. I stayed at an ancient house not far from the Rue des Tonneliers, right in the heart of this queer, timeless old city, and, there, I was told a very eerie story connected with some very strange bones now in the "dry" section of a certain Belgian Medical Museum. The ancient house had formerly belonged to the order of the Black Friars, or Dominican monks; but, about 1908, it had been acquired by a private person who let out flats in it to artists, or to foreigners desiring to make a protracted stay in this picturesque old Flemish town. As would be expected of a former monastic institution, the house had grim and massive walls, many small rooms that had once been cells, tortuous stone stairways, and very narrow passages.

But there had been complaints about the place. People came and rented the rooms and flats, for which only a modest rental was asked; but many of them packed up and left, some even before their period of paid occupancy had ended. There had been stories of eerie footsteps of something unseen ascending the stairs, not merely in the night, but in the day. One Englishman, who was about to come out of his door on a top story, hurriedly shut it when he saw, in the dim angle of the stone passage outside, where only a crepuscular light entered even at sunny noon, what he called some "damned inhuman," but vague and bizarre object, standing and waiting. He could not make out what it was, but it shuffled and padded off, leaving behind a horrible stench, as "if it had come out of the

Devil's own latrine!" There were also eerie raps on doors, and when the doors opened, no one was seen there.

At last, the *patron*, who saw that if these phenomena continued, he would be left with an empty house on his hands—since not even the most downright skeptic can be prevailed on to live and spend his days and nights in an old house which has "something queer about it"—got in some builder's hefty men and had them break up the heavy stone flags of a very ancient and roomy stone cellar, which was believed to be the source of the phenomena. They did not find any coffins, or skeletons under the floor, nor any fruits of the clandestine armors of medieval monks and nuns, nor any sign that someone in the fourteenth or fifteenth century had by some means "raised the Devil" and couldn't get him to lie down afterwards! But when the laborers were asked to apply their chisels, and picks and crowbars to the thick *walls* of this queer cellar, they opened up something on which no pathologist could express a decided opinion. They found, right in the middle of the thick cellar-wall, a sort of alcove in which were strange bones that did not look human.

THE PATHOLOGIST SHUDDERS

A surgeon, who was also a pathologist, was called in, and when he examined the bones, even he, hardened to macabre sights, shuddered. He said: "This must have been some monstrosity, walled up untold years ago, and the bones all belong to the same uncanny being. *Nom du diable* . . . I confess I am unable to express an opinion on the origin of this horrible thing; nor can anyone now say if the monks knew anything about it."

All one can say is that the monstrosity was not an infant, but adult; and whether or not it was the fault of some nasty amour of the unnatural type denounced in the books of the Pentateuch, or the remains of some horrible thing teleported to Bruges from some world in space, it is beyond the wit of man to determine. All *I* can say, besides this, is that the Flemish gentleman who told me this story, and who now owns the old house, assured me that there are now no raps on doors by an unseen thing, nor charnel-house stenches; but that all is now as holy and quiet there, as the nave of a church consecrated with holy water. I had no inclination to test his assurance; but, after cogitating "Who had done the walling-up and when?" I made tracks for a cheery pavement café off the *Grande*

Place and called for an extra large glass of strong schnapps. It is obvious that a number of persons unknown could have told a most hair-raising story about what went on in that ancient cellar!

THE SKELETON IN THE CYLINDER

In all my varied experience as a newspaperman investigating mysteries, I have never, except in the case of the enigma of Bruges, come across a weirder story than that of the "Skeleton in the Cylinder." This Grand Guignolesque thriller opened on a summer day in the last year of the Second World War, 1945, when some U.S. soldiers were running a bulldozer over a bombed site, behind a Methodist chapel in Liverpool. They had returned to quarters for the night when a man strolled on to the site and casually poked about among the debris. His attention was attracted by a peculiar cylinder which he could not force open. He told the police, who got a mechanic to prise off some iron bolts and rivets. They made a macabre discovery. Inside the cylinder was the partly decomposed corpse of a man, lying on dirty sacking. He had evidently lain there a long time, for part of the cranium was missing, although hair still adhered to the skull.

A closer examination disclosed what appeared to be diaries, and one of the entries read: "June 1885 . . . meeting . . . 1 P.M., F. C. Grady . . . at Cons."

There were other papers, including five account sheets, all badly decayed. On one sheet there could be made out the name of a firm: "T.C. Williams and Co., Leeds Street, Liverpool," and a truncated date: "18 . . ." The police who, it must be said, did not appear to make a very good job of the investigations, recorded for the coroner at the inquest that: "A postcard was found on the body, bearing the name of T.C. Williams, and written by a man named A.E. Harris on 3 July, 1885. The postmark was blurred and cannot be deciphered. There was a handkerchief, not marked with initials or laundry signs. Also a worn signet ring, hallmarked 'London 1859.' No money was in the corpse's pockets, and no other valuables. A brooch was also found in the cylinder."

The coroner's inquest returned an open verdict, and the coroner said it was impossible to ascertain the cause of death, which might have happened sixty years ago. "I do not doubt," he sapiently said, "that the man had crawled into the cylinder. He wore clothing of good mid-Victorian quality."

A PERFECT MURDER?

"Crawled into the cylinder?" Why? On the face of it, this affair has the air of being a perfect murder veiled by the passage of many years Why, too, did not the Liverpool C.I.D. examine the Liverpool newspaper and directories of the year 1885 and 1886, to be found in one national library and accessible, if not at the British Museum Newspaper Library, certainly at Liverpool newspaper offices, to which common law gives right of access to police or public. It is likely, too, that if a man had been reported missing in Liverpool in 1885 or 1886, the police would have had a record of him, and he may have been the man with the name of "A.E. Harris." Was any relative or descendant of T.C. Williams of this concern still alive in 1945? If so, it does not appear that the Liverpool police exerted themselves to find out; nor did the coroner make any obvious comments. Suppose, too, that "A.E. Harris" did *not* crawl into the cylinder, as this coroner suggested, but was *pushed into it*—which is consonant with the obvious deduction that "A.E. Harris," or the man who became a corpse, could hardly have bolted himself into the cylinder? Here are all the elements of a mystery that would have delighted Sherlock Holmes, and have rightly called down from him some sardonic comments on both police and coroner. Admittedly, it is unlikely that a suspect or suspects might still be alive.

UFOs Attack Earth . . . The Out of Control Universe of Harold T. Wilkins

Quantum Physics And Bizarre Animals

One hesitates to overuse the word "prescient," but once again Harold T. Wilkins, writing in the 1950s, seems way ahead of the game in regards to the new Quantum Physics and its implications for paranormal research. The idea did not begin to catch on with the general public until sometime in the 1980s, when nearly everyone began to hear bantered about some of the extraordinary findings that were leading mainstream physicists to conjecture about things like parallel universes, the kind of "otherworldliness" that can now be drawn as equations on a chalkboard. As we scrutinize these pages from *Strange Mysteries of Time and Space,* we can see Wilkins does a marvelous job of using the advances in science to theorize about teleportation, and tells the famous story of nineteenth century farmer David Lang, who disappeared completely one summer afternoon, in full view of his family and other witnesses, into an unknown dimension from which he could not return. Stories of monstrous animals that may enter our world from another dimension and wreak havoc are also recounted here, and even a 13th century debunker has a say as well.

⚜ ⚜ ⚜

Our mid-twentieth century age of nuclear fission and thermonuclear fission, radar, television, electronics and the special and general relativity theories associated with Einstein, have brought us to the theoretical pass where an atomic particle may behave as a wave one minute, and a particle the next; so that the physicist is driven to call in the metaphysics of Kant and the "unknowable noumenon" in order to arrive at even a temporary hypothesis about the nature of man, mind, matter and the universe.

The scientist is like the man who consulted the old sea god, Proteus, who was difficult of access and often refused to give an answer to a problem. He assumed different shapes if not properly secured in fetters, and, in the end, vanished in a flame of fire, a whirlwind, or a rushing stream.

THE FUSION OF PHYSICS WITH METAPHYSICS

Nature, as Bertrand Russell has said, presents us with "the wave with nothing to wave in." It ought not, therefore, to arouse derision or undue skepticism if one adumbrates, or prophesies that, for science, a time is rapidly approaching when the scientist willy-nilly, may have to attempt a fusion of physics and metaphysics, which will bring him into contact with the uncomfortable and mysterious worlds of the fourth dimension, whose plane lies at right angles or, sometimes, seems parallel to our own everyday world of three dimensions. Our world which that other very mysterious world seems, at times, to interpenetrate.

There is, so to speak, "a hole in the wall," or, to vary the metaphor, the occurrence of a vortex in matter-energy through which certain people of all social classes and ranks, animals, and objects, involuntarily and unexpectedly may pass, and from which there may, or may *not* be a return to the world from which they were "teleported." If they do return, it will usually be found that the experience of this weird phenomenon is accompanied by amnesia, entire forgetfulness of what happened just before, during and after the phenomenon.

This weird phenomenon is not an abstract affair, but is, has and will be connected with the mysterious disappearances of people in cases where no normally physical or criminological explanation can be found. In order, however dimly and very imperfectly to conceive what happens when a man or woman, an animal, or object vanishes from the third into the fourth dimension of the continuum of space-time, we may assume the hypothesis of a two-dimensional object, with length and breadth, being lifted up into the third dimension of height, and so transcending the bounds of the circle which confined it. It would be re-deposited again in the two-dimensional plane outside the circle, and so, after it had vanished, it would reappear, mysteriously, at another point in space.

FINDING THE WAY BACK

Or, again, if the object, or actor, were the norm of our own world of three-dimensions, such an object or actor, passing into the four-dimensional world might, and very often might *not*, come back from that unknown and mysterious bourne to which he or it had been teleported.

To pass through the "hole in the wall," or the warp, or crack, or vortex, or rift, in space, the sentient object, the man or woman, may require to have a functional peculiarity, or unconscious or subconscious "knack," which the learned Victorian, F.W.H. Myers, called "psychorrhagic diathesis," by which, in conditions we do not yet know produces a breaking-through of the stuff of mind-energy-matter and may affect a sort of inversion of the space-time continuum. The actor falls through the warp, or vortex, in space, somewhat in the way a swimmer may be carried away by a current under ice, in a lake, or a floe, and, thereafter, he may, or may *not* rediscover the point of entry. If he does not, the world from which he mysteriously vanished will know him no more!

The phenomenon may be a two-way one. It may involve an involuntary, unexpected and certainly undesired transference or teleportation from our own three-dimensional world to the unknown one of four dimensions, or even vice-versa. One may conceive, as, indeed, the relativity theory suggests, that worlds may exist not, as we empirically suppose, in succession, but side by side, one being invisible to the other, and connected with it only through a space vortex, or the "hole in the wall in space-time."

The strange phenomena recorded in this book were and are not confined to the nineteenth and twentieth centuries, or to any age in the past or present, but were experienced in the early and later Middle Ages, and, naturally, misinterpreted according to theological preconceptions.

They *were*, however, recorded often by learned monastics who have been smiled and laughed at for their pains and their "superstition." And, no doubt, the phenomena occurred in the earlier ages of Egypt, Babylonia, Sumeria, India, Rome and Greece, or Carthaginia and Etruria. They belong to every age, in fact.

UFOs Attack Earth ... The Out of Control Universe of Harold T. Wilkins

PULLED INTO THE VOID

We may preface accounts of these weird and bizarre phenomena with a brief narrative of a strange incident that occurred no longer ago than the afternoon of 23 September, 1880. I summarize from various contemporary newspapers in the U.S.A.:

On that afternoon, a man named David Lang, who had a farm about twelve miles from the small township of Gallatin, in Sumner County, Tennessee, spoke to his wife and two children on the veranda of their farmhouse, and, in sight of them, walked across a forty acre field and was never seen again. As Lang was walking across this pasture-field of close-cropped grass, an attorney and Lang's brother-in-law were driving up a lane, in a buggy, towards the farmhouse. The attorney saw Lang in the middle of the field, and was about to shout to him—and there were no hedges, trees, boulders, or fences at or near the spot—when, to the attorney's amazement, Lang vanished from sight instantaneously, as if the earth had suddenly opened and swallowed him up! The alarmed wife and the two men at once went to the spot, found no crack in the turf, or soil, and nothing whatever to indicate what had happened or where Lang had gone. One moment, Lang was, the next he was *not*! Every inch of the field was searched by the police, but with no result. A surveyor and a geologist said that limestone bedrock lay a few feet under the soil, and no crack of fissure could be found in it. The search went on for a month, all in vain!

A year later—and this has reference to one's point that there may often be "no return" to our own world, for the luckless actor, or patient!—a very strange thing occurred.

On a day in early August, 1881, the missing man's boy and girl were walking over this field, when they noticed that the grass at the spot where their father had mysteriously disappeared showed a 20-feet wide circle of high and rank grass. All outside the circle had been cropped by sheep, or grazed by cattle; but no cow, or sheep, or horse would venture into the circle, not even a cricket or a grasshopper. They would not approach it, but shied away in fear. For some reason, the girl was impelled to shout out: "Father, are you anywhere around?"

UFOs Attack Earth... The Out of Control Universe of Harold T. Wilkins

She repeated the inquiry four times, and the boy joined in. No reply came, and then they were about to walk away, thinking how silly they were, when, of a sudden, they heard a voice call for help. It seemed faint and faraway—in, but not of this world! The startled mother was told. She went to the spot in the field, and called, and her husband answered. They went back for several days; but each day the voice grew fainter, and at last was heard no more.

It seemed that Lang, wherever he was, or had been precipitated, could not find the point of reentry to the world of three dimensions.

ANIMALS FROM ANOTHER DIMENSION?

Besides phenomena which seem to relate to teleportation of human beings, the ages of faith have, in many records known only to highly specialized scholars, or to Orientalists, told of the appearance of animals or monsters, apparently unknown to zoologists or herpetologists. Often the stories are passed over with a smile or a scoff as just travelers' tales. However, in this chapter, that need not deter us from mentioning some of them. Abu Hassan al-Masudi, an Arab historian and geographer, descendant of one of the Prophet's companions and native of Baghdad, traveled in China, India, Egypt, Persia and the Caspian region, in or about the year of the Hegira 332 (A.D. 946), and tells, in his *Meadows of Gold*, about an adventure of one, er Rashid:

"One day, he was hunting in the country, near el-Mausil, when a white falcon in his hand became uneasy, and he let it go. After a long time, it came back with an insect like a serpent, or a fish, with wings like fins. Some observers have told me that, in Egypt and other countries, they have seen white serpents in the air, moving from place to place as fast as lightning; that they lit sometimes on an animal and killed it; and that they are sometimes heard flying by night, when, in their locomotion in the air, they are accompanied by a noise like that made when new cloth is unfolded. Persons who have no knowledge of the subject and superstitious are heard to say that the sound proceeds from witches flying on quails' wings. But it seems to prove that animals live in the upper elements."

This oddity would have appealed to the late Sir Arthur Conan Doyle! The Chronicon of Denys de Tell-Mahre, a patriarch of the Syrian Jacobites, who was born in Mesopotamia (Iraq) about the end of the eighth century A.D. records as follows:

A.D. 774: "Before the reign of the (Byzantine-Greek) Emperor Leo IV (that is, prior to A.D. 774), there raged a plague, followed by the appearance of frightening and terrible animals who feared nothing and no man. They fled from no man and, indeed, killed many. A very little they were like wolves, but their muzzle was small and long, and they had great ears, like those of horses. The skin on their dorsal spine resembled the bristles of pigs, and stuck straight up. These mysterious animals committed great ravages on the people in the Abdin Rock region, near Hoh. In certain villages, they devoured more than 100 people, and in many others, from twenty and forty to fifty. Nothing could be done against them for they were fearless of man. If, by chance, men pursued them, in no wise did the monsters become scared or flee, but turned on the men. If men loosed their weapons on a monster, it leapt on the men and tore them in pieces.

"These monsters entered houses and yards, and seized and carried off children, and went out, no one offering resistance. They climbed in the night on to terraces, abducted children from their beds, and went off before any could oppose them. When they appeared, the dogs did not bark, so that for this reason alone the countryside suffered a more bitter experience than it had ever known before. Two or three men dared not move around together, and no more were cattle seen in the fields, for all had been devoured by these monsters. Indeed, when one of them attacked a herd of goats, or flock of sheep, it took away several at a time. These monsters passed into Arzanene (a region in southern Armenia, on the borders of Assyria H.T.W.) and badly ravaged every village, as well as in the country of Maipherk and on Mt. Cahai, and they caused damage at Amida." (On the upper Tigris. Several pages are here missing in the original manuscript. H.T.W.)

What were these strange animals, and whence did they come?

DEMONS WHO COME WITH THE WIND

The Chronicon of Frodoardus—he is named, variously, as Frodardus, Flordardus, or Flavellus, was born in A.D. 894 at Epernay, and became a regular Benedictine monk, writing his Chronicon at the mature age of seventy in A.D.

963—tells of a phenomenon several times recorded in the following six centuries, in England and France—and still as mysterious today:

A.D. 943: "Exceedingly great tempest and whirlwind completely overthrew very old and very strongly built houses of cement on the hills of the Martyrs (Montmartre, Paris) where Saint Denys was martyred. It was reported that things like demons or horses were seen at the height of the storm, which struck a church, destroying the beams and removing walls, and laid waste all with the vines on the hills."

Some people in America, today, would suggest that these so-called "demon horses" may have been flying saucers!

Abbot Ralph of Coggeshall Abbey, Essex, has, in his Chronicle, a very odd story of another phenomenon in a storm, *not* of a type appealing to modern meteorologists, zoologists, or marine biologists:

24 June, 1205: "In the holy night of John the Baptist, all night thunder roared and lightning, terrific, incessantly flashed all over England. A certain strange monster was struck by lightning at Maidstone, in Kent, where, in the highest degree, the most horrible thunder reverberated. This monster had the head of an ass, the belly of a human being, and other monstrous members and limbs of animals very unlike each other. Its black corpse was scorched by the lightning, and so intolerable a stench came from it that hardly anyone was able to go near it."

As to the last feature, any modern farm-worker, hardened to the foul smell of silo-pits, could have managed the approach to an interesting animal that may remind us that Loch Ness monsters, or what the Irish call "piastes," are not necessarily merely the products of imagination and overworked Scottish or Irish distilleries.

(I, myself, and another man, saw, on Tuesday, 5 July, 1949, at 11:30 A.M., an even weirder sight in the creek of East Looe, at Cornwall. A young news editor of the *Daily Mail* promised to investigate this, but did not do so. Two remarkable saurians, 19-20 feet long, with bottle-green heads one behind the other, their middle parts under the water of the tidal creek of East Looe, apparently chasing a shoal of fish up the creek. What was amazing were their dorsal parts: ridged, serrated, and like the old Chinese pictures of dragons. Gulls swooped down towards the one in the rear, which had a large piece of orange peel on his dorsal parts. These monsters—and two of us saw them—resembled the plesiosaurus of Mesozoic times. In that month of 1949, the Gulf Stream showed an aberration from its normal course; so that fishermen at Mevagissey, not far away, were scared when they netted a 20-foot-long tropical turtle, never seen, normally, off Cornwall. Unfortunately, I had left my camera behind. It is futile to report such phenomena to marine biological stations. H.T.W.)

WAR IN THE SKIES

Abbot Ralph records another eerie incident, in a violent electrical storm, on 29 July, of the same year, 1205:

"In the night of the festival of the holy martyr, Felix, horrible thunders and cracklings and incessant lightning raged all over England, all night long; so that one thought the Day of Judgment had come. Men nearly died of fear and horror. Men, women and cattle were killed, houses burned to ashes, corn crushed flat, with great stones the size of goose eggs, with sharp stings. Trees torn up by the roots and carried to other places. Ropes appeared, as if whirled around and some torn to pieces right in the middle.

"Next day, certain monstrous tracks were seen in several places, and of a kind never seen before. Men said they were the prints of demons."

The abbot seeks to explain this phenomenon as a "war in the skies," in which "good angels" cut "demons to pieces and thrust them into chasms in the earth."

He says: "The philosophers care to dispute this more than other high matters."

UFOs Attack Earth . . . The Out of Control Universe of Harold T. Wilkins

A Final Vanishing Act

We close with more stories from *Strange Mysteries of Time and Space*, two intriguing tales of pilots gone missing. The first story, about American airman Paul Redfern, has echoes of the classic 1979 movie "Apocalypse Now," in which the marooned white man is taken for a god by the local natives, who nevertheless threaten him with becoming their next supper if he refuses the honor. Quite naturally opting to live as a god, Redfern is never seen or heard from again. The story of William Brophy ends this book with the haunting image of the lost pilot walking the beach of a poorly charted island, peopled only by savages, and not reachable by any boat due to extremely rough coral reefs. It is a portrait of loneliness and regret that again showcases Harold T. Wilkins' way with a story, something both strange and bizarre and yet poignantly human.

⚜ ⚜ ⚜

Old Davy Jones, with his locker, runs a neck and neck race with Daedalus and his flying coffin in the Great Mystery Stakes, and one in which the "unplumbed, salt, estranging sea" and the recesses of lonely mountains offer no prizes; for there are no "winners" in *this* race. A skeleton whose bones lie across the blade of a propeller, or whose skull peers out from the instrument panel in the cockpit of a shattered plane in a wood, or high up on the rugged flanks of a towering mountain, or in the col of a corridor walled in by frowning precipices, or on the edge of a green glacier, may be the only clue to some years-old mystery, forgotten by all save the relatives or wives of lost men.

A PILOT SAYS GOODBYE

In the summer of 1928, an American airman, Paul Redfern, kissed his pretty wife goodbye, taxied down the sands of Brunswick, Georgia, and took off into the skies on an exceedingly foolish stunt trip to Brazil. His plane had only one engine, a death trap if anything untimely befell him, and he was alone on a journey of 4,700 miles. The months passed into years and his wife gave him up for dead; for the last news she had was the report of a Hollander skipper of an oil tanker who had seen a plane streaking across the skies off the coast of Dutch Guiana. In that year airlines were in their infancy, and planes in those waters were not the commonplace they have since become. Rio de Janeiro cabled that no one in Brazil had seen or heard of Redfern or his plane.

TO LIVE AS A GOD OR NOT AT ALL

Then, in 1933, an engineer and explorer, Charles Hasler, came in from the green hell of the Amazon wilderness, to Manaos, where he told a very odd story:

"Far up in the jungles of Amazonas, somewhere near the Rio Putumayo, a savage tribe of headhunting Indians have a new chief who has become a god. It seems that he has a white skin, and one day there flew into the open space of the *aldeia*, with its cannibal cooking pots, of burnt-clay, a 'great bird,' which roared over the treetops and landed in a clearing. The 'bird' came from the northeast. At once the headhunters deposed their chief and elected what they took to be a mightier man. The new arrival was a modest man, and tried to decline the honor; but the headhunters would not take no for an answer. The witch doctor gave a sly smile and the pupils of his black wizened eyes contracted. He indicated the cooking pots. The great bird-man could choose: either godship or *that*! Anyway, if they could not have a live god, they would elect to have a trophy—the white bird-man's head—to hang under the black beams of the tribal lodge! The new arrival chose, reluctantly, to become the Indians' god. But, while, they fed him on the fat of the Indian land, they saw to it that he had no chance to walk out on them and ramble into the great forest."

Home at faraway Brunswick, Georgia, pretty Mrs. Redfern was overjoyed, and she passed the glad news to Paul Redfern's father, while Mrs. Redfern, the mother, said she had always had a feeling that Paul was alive, and would one day return. An expedition was organized; but alas, they could not find the "white god," or Redfern! It may be said that these stories of white men held prisoners and well treated by the Indians, short of letting them go, are not uncommon in the Matto Grosso, or up the little-known Rio Branco.

In the case of missing planes equipped with rafts or lifebelts, it has been found that devilish man-eating sharks will follow survivors for days, trying persistently to get their horny backs under the rafts or appliances, and lever or tip the castaways off into the sea! It was in July 1937 that gallant Amelia Earhart flew from Lae, New Guinea, bound for the lonely mid-Pacific Howland Island, on the equator. She never arrived, and sea and air searches found no trace of her, her navigator, nor any wreckage. A similar baffling mystery surrounds the fate of William Brophy, an Englishman, who in 1932 attempted a foolish solo flight from Manila, in the Philippines, to Shanghai, not then barred off by Chinese Communists. His route was over the South China Sea, not well-charted, even today, and thronged with little, unknown islands and sown with rock pinnacles of coral.

LOST AND ALL ALONE

There is some reason to suppose that Brophy was, later, sighted and left to his fate. Follows a letter sent to me by a correspondent in Manila:

"Brophy took a mascot with him for luck: a puppy. It did not help him any! A story has been cabled here from Yokohama about a Japanese skipper of a lugger, who, in August 1933, about seventeen months after Brophy took off for China, was passing by the rocky coast of the wild and solitary island of Yami, a practically inaccessible island, some way out beyond the northern end of Luzon. In the dusk, he saw a white man, with a dog, wandering on the beach of Yami. Only untamed savages live there. The man was looking out to sea and waving a piece of cloth in the direction of the lugger. The Japanese man focused his telescope on to the beach and made out the figure of a man, in rags and tatters, signaling for help. The Japanese man swore that the coral reefs made an attempt at landing too dangerous. So he steamed on and left the poor guy to his fate. Yami is mountainous, and the savages have a bad reputation. I know nobody who has ever landed there, and little or nothing is known of the place, which is about 150 miles from Aparri, in Luzon. I guess the poor devil will stay there, unless some of Uncle Sam's airmen can reach him."

UFOs Attack Earth . . . The Out of Control Universe of Harold T. Wilkins

The Great Unknown

Harold T. Wilkins left behind a body of work that has yet to find the vast and dedicated audience it deserves. Hopefully this book will have a small part in changing that situation. Wilkins was not only a genius at collecting and telling stories that floated in from the great unknown; he was also a visionary who tapped into the wellsprings of the future even as he laid some of the groundwork for the future of Ufology and paranormal research in general.

As a testament to his levelheaded conservatism of approach, one marvels at how much of what he wrote is so seamlessly consistent with discoveries made in our own time, which he seemed to prophesy so accurately and with such intelligent foresight.

And there is of course the sheer beauty of his writing, which ranges from a delicate, gentlemanly sense of humor to a wonderfully engaging descriptive style to a determined stickler armed with the indisputable facts. Everything one enjoys about good paranormal writing is here in abundance.

We can only conclude that when the mysteries recounted herein are finally solved, when answers come from somewhere we cannot yet imagine, that Harold T. Wilkins will be standing shyly there, in the background, telling himself it was worth the wait.

--Sean Casteel

UFOs Attack Earth . . . The Out of Control Universe of Harold T. Wilkins

Mr. UFO: Timothy Green Beckley (below) and Sean Casteel (above)